# Fabrics for Needlework

By the same author
Needlework
Making Curtains, Cushions and Covers

Rosalie P. Giles holds City and Guilds 1st Class Teacher's Certificates in Dressmaking, Needlework and Cookery. The author was formerly the lecturer in charge of Dress in the Home Economics Department of the Norwich City College

# FABRICS FOR NEEDLEWORK

## Rosalie Giles

Methuen Educational
London Toronto Sydney Wellington

First published in Great Britain 1962
by Methuen & Co Ltd
Reprinted (with minor corrections) 1963
Second edition published 1964
Third edition published 1970
Reprinted 1970 and 1973
Fourth (metric) edition 1977
by Methuen Educational
11 New Fetter Lane, London EC4P 4EE
Copyright © 1962, 1964, 1970 and 1976
Rosalie P. Giles
Printed in Great Britain by
Cox & Wyman Ltd.
Fakenham Norfolk

School edition ISBN O 423 89870 1
Library edition ISBN O 423 89880 9

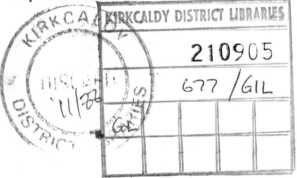

# Contents

# Foreword

As so many books about fabrics are very technical I have tried to keep this one as simple as possible as my aim is to help those students who are studying for G.C.E. and other dressmaking and needlework examinations. I hope that it may also help the housewife who wishes to know how fabrics are made and how she should use and look after them.

I am very grateful to the British Man-made Fibres Federation, Imperial Chemical Industries Ltd. and the British Nylon Spinners Ltd. for kindly allowing me to reproduce their flow charts, and to the Calico Printers' Association for information on various finishes and their care and to Courtaulds Ltd. for much help with man-made fibres.

Also I am much indebted to Mr. G.C. Gregory for all the care and trouble he took when making the micro-photographs of the different fabrics and to Coe Commercial Photographers for those of lace.

# 1 Why We Need Fabrics

Have you ever stopped to think what our lives would be like if we had no fabrics? There would be no clothes to flatter us, keep us warm or to protect us from the scorching rays of the sun — no towels with which to dry ourselves after a swim or bath — no curtains for the windows nor coverings for our furniture and floors — in fact very little comfort at all. In the times in which we live we could not do without fabrics, so let us look a little more closely into the reasons why we need them so much.

## 1. KEEPING COOL

One of the more important reasons for wearing clothing is to keep the temperature of the body even. In good health this should be 36.9°C and we keep this steady partly through the food we eat, which burns up inside us as coal burns on a fire, and partly through the skin. We can lose heat through the skin because in it there are millions of sweat glands which open out on to the surface and when we become overheated these glands open wide to let perspiration flow out of them on to the skin, where it dries. Now, in order to dry, perspiration needs heat, so it takes it away from the body and we cool down. You can prove this for yourselves by pouring a few drops of a quick-drying liquid, such as methylated spirit or eau-de-Cologne, on to your skin. Notice how cool you feel as it dries.

On very hot days or in tropical climates when we feel uncomfortably hot the sweat glands work overtime pouring out perspiration so that it can dry by taking heat from us and from the surrounding air. To keep cool under these conditions we must wear fabrics which will protect us from the sun and, at the same time, soak up perspiration and dry quickly. Some materials can do this better than others, linens and cottons for example, and we say they are *good conductors* of heat because they allow it to escape from the body.

We can become overheated during strenuous exercise, such as playing games, and once again we perspire. If the day is cool, all the heat needed to dry the perspiration is taken from the body, and none from the surrounding air, and should we sit about in this state we may cool down too quickly and get a chill, unless we put on some extra clothing to absorb the moisture and slow down the cooling process. Again some fabrics are better for this purpose than others. Wool, silk and rayons are the best as they can absorb moisture and hold it so that it evaporates slowly, and when they become slightly damp these particular materials gain extra warmth so that we do not feel chilly.

Colour also plays its part in keeping us cool. White repels heat and reflects it back, whereas black attracts and absorbs it. This is why, in hot climates, people

1

wear white and light colours to keep cool. It used to be the custom in cooler climates to wear dark colours in the winter to attract warmth, but nowadays with better heating systems, not quite so much attention is paid to this.

## 2.  KEEPING WARM

The air in a room which has no ventilation becomes stuffy and quite still and its temperature remains even, but the moment doors and windows are opened, cool air from outside blows in and the warm air from inside moves out making the room cooler. From this we can see that when air is perfectly still it will keep warm, it is only when it moves about that we feel draughts. It is rather like being in a bath which is not quite warm enough; so long as one lies perfectly still it is not too bad but the smallest movement makes it feel chilly round the edges. Therefore we can understand that if it is possible to trap a layer of warm, perfectly still air round the body by means of fabrics and keep it there, we will feel warm however cold the air around us is. The still air acts as an insulator. Knitted, woolly, hairy, fluffy or fur fabrics are able to trap and hold pockets of still air in between the fluffy fibres and this is why we find them warm to wear. We call them *bad conductors* of heat because they help to prevent the body losing heat. Apart from the pockets of air which are held all over the material these fabrics trap more air between one garment and another. For instance, if you wear a woollen vest, the fine hairs all over the fabric will hold it a little away from your skin, forming a layer of air between the vest and you. This air becomes warm from the heat of the body and remains so. If, over the vest you wear a woolly jumper, a further layer of air is trapped and held between the vest and the jumper and you will feel warmer still. From this you will see that clothes should be fairly loose to hold air between them. If they are tight there is no room for the air and they will be less warm. It is not the thickness of the fabric which matters so much as the amount of air it can hold. A cardigan very closely knitted in thick wool may not be so warm to wear as one more loosely knitted in fine wool, as the larger spaces between the looser stitches will hold more air than stitches which are so close as to have little space between them. When we put that extra blanket on the bed in cold weather, it is not so much the extra thickness we need but the extra layer of still air which is trapped underneath it. An eiderdown is so warm because a large amount of air is entangled in the feathers filling it and the warmth of a quilt depends on the air caught up in between two or three layers of fabric which are stitched loosely together in a pattern to hold it there. Quilted bed-jackets and dressing-gowns usually have the middle layer made of cotton wool or wadding which consist of thousands of short cotton (and nowadays polyester) fibres held loosely together with pockets of air between them.

We have just read how the loose weaving of a hairy yarn plays an important part in keeping us warm. Now, the very close weaving of a smooth yarn can also keep us warm but in a different way. Whereas a woollen jersey is worn to *keep warmth in,* a windcheater is worn to *keep cold out.* Windcheaters are often made from cotton, which, remember, is a good conductor of heat, but the yarn used to make the fabric is very fine and the weaving extremely close, making the spaces between the threads so minute that air cannot pass through them easily. The fabric is not intended to contribute warmth but to be a covering through which wind cannot penetrate. Nylon raincoats will serve the same purpose and plastic ones are even better, because plastic material is completely dense and no air whatever can pass through it. However, of the three, finely woven cotton is probably the most comfortable to wear, as cotton is absorbent, whereas nylon yarn and plastic are waterproof and therefore cannot soak up perspiration (which, being unable to dry out inside, remains moist on the skin and then bacteria attack it, causing it to smell offensive), although on the outer side they absorb little moisture and dry quickly.

From all you have read up to this point you should be able to draw the following conclusions:

| If a yarn is: | The fabric should be: |
|---|---|
| *a)* smooth | a good conductor of heat and cool |
| *b)* reasonably absorbent | to wear |
| *c)* quick to dry | |
| *d)* woven with a loose or medium weave | |
| | |
| *a)* hairy | |
| *b)* absorbent | a bad conductor of heat and warm |
| *c)* slow drying | to wear |
| *d)* loosely woven | |
| | |
| *a)* very fine | |
| *b)* extremely closely woven | probably windproof and comfortable |
| *c)* absorbent | to wear |
| | |
| *a)* very fine | windproof and waterproof |
| | |
| *a)* very fine | windproof and waterproof. Not so |
| *b)* very closely woven | comfortable to wear as perspiration |
| *c)* not absorbent | cannot evaporate |

## 3. KEEPING DRY

When some yarns absorb moisture they swell up and fill completely any spaces between them in a woven fabric. Cotton and linen yarns are able to do this and have the added advantage of becoming stronger when they are wet. Therefore they are used for making fabrics for awnings, tents, sailcloth and fire hoses. The yarn used is coarse and woven extremely closely, as in the case of windcheaters, so that wind cannot penetrate. When it rains, the yarn absorbs just so much moisture to enable it to swell and make the fabric dense enough to cause rain to glance off it instead of driving through it. Nowadays the fabric is probably treated with a waterproofing finish as well, just to make quite sure it will stand up to severe conditions. Apart from keeping out wind and rain, the fabric will hold off the sun's rays and provide shade. Tents can become rather stuffy and airless because fresh air cannot get through the dense weave. Nylon is also suitable for windcheaters as the very fine yarn can be so closely woven that it is windproof and water-repellent besides being lightweight and very strong. Both nylon and polyester are used extensively for tents.

Some woollen yarns are naturally water-repellent. If you have ever been out in the rain wearing a woollen coat, you may have noticed how the raindrops cling to the ends of the hairy fibres without penetrating the material and can be shaken off. For this reason closely woven wool gabardine is often used for making showerproof raincoats, the hairy fibres hold off the rain and the close weave prevents penetration for quite a long time. This does not mean that the coat is waterproof, because it is not, but it will afford satisfactory protection if you are caught in a shower. The coats are usually given a water-repelling treatment for added protection, but they are not meant to be worn in a continuous downpour, as eventually the water will get through. The only raincoats which are really waterproof are those made from rubber, plastic or oilskin. Seamen's socks and jerseys are made from oiled wool because oil and water do not mix and if wool is treated with oil it will repel water.

A different way of keeping dry is with the use of towels, not a question of keeping water out but of getting rid of moisture which is already present. The terry towelling we use for drying ourselves after a bath has to be made from a fibre which will absorb quite a lot of moisture and dry quickly. The fabric must be strong when it is wet and have a rough surface. The roughness is important for two reasons. (1) The shaggy loops woven into the base fabric all over the surface help to absorb more moisture. (2) After a hot bath the sweat glands are open wide and we are losing heat. The friction of the rough towel brings extra blood to the surface of the skin and stops us cooling down too quickly. This works in the reverse way also, because after a swim when we are cold the sweat glands close up (giving us 'goose flesh') so that perspiration cannot come out of them to dry and take heat away from us. A brisk rub with a rough towel brings the blood to the surface and makes us glow with warmth.

When we dry dishes we need a different kind of towel. It has to be absorbent, strong when wet, quick to dry, hardwearing, capable of being boiled to sterilize it and it must have a smooth surface, free from lint so that no fluff is left on glass or china. Linen is ideal for this, but recently tea towels made from terry towelling have become popular. Linen and cotton are the yarns most suitable for making towels as they have all the qualities needed. Absorbency is very important. Just try wiping a wet dish with nylon material and see how you get on!

Having found out how to keep dry, let us discuss getting wet — in swim suits. The ideal fabric to wear for a swim suit on a cold day is undoubtedly made from wool. It will hold air to keep you warm, absorb moisture which evaporates slowly and become warmer when it is wet. Therefore you are less likely to get a chill. However, the gaily patterned and beautifully styled cotton swim suits are very attractive. Really they are most suitable for wearing in hot weather as the moisture which cotton absorbs dries quickly, withdrawing heat from the body. It is unwise to lie about in a wet cotton swim suit unless the day is excessively hot, when you may come to no harm.

## 4. PROTECTIVE CLOTHING

Yet another reason for wearing clothes is to give protection when we do dirty jobs or handle harmful materials such as chemicals or electrical apparatus. Clothes are worn also in the interests of hygiene as in the case of doctors, nurses or people who handle food, so that germs may not infect others. Fabrics for these purposes must be hardwearing and, in most cases, able to stand up to repeated laundering and even boiling to sterilize them. Cotton and linen are very suitable. Nylon and polyester fibres are widely used for overalls as both wash easily and the latter resists chemicals.

Rubber, although not really a fabric, is used for medical purposes and for gloves because it is dense and germs cannot get through it. It is a non-conductor of electricity and is useful as a protection when handling electrical apparatus.

Plastic, again not really a fabric, protects food from germs and household pests, and other fabrics from moth grubs.

## 5. CLOTHES FOR SUPPORT

Roll-ons and pantie-girdles support the tummy and give one a better shape, providing a smooth foundation for outer wear. For such garments it is necessary to use a fabric which will give support without restricting the body movements. Such fabrics are made from elastane yarns which have taken the place of the former rubber-based elastic fabrics.

## 6. CLOTHES FOR ADORNMENT

Since time began people have delighted in 'dressing up', and why not? If you wear dowdy clothes you feel dull, but how good you feel when you look nice!

It is very uplifting, so by all means make your clothes as attractive and becoming as they are functional and sensible. There is no reason at all, for example, why a macintosh, besides keeping out the rain, should not be gay and exciting and attractively cut — if it has to serve a dismal purpose, let it look good and then you won't mind the rain so much!

# 2 From Fibre to Yarn

Because fabrics are so necessary to us it is important to understand how they are made so that we know how to care for them and for what purpose each kind is most suitable. Remember that:

a) Most fabrics are made from yarn, woven or knitted, stitched or felted.

b) Yarns are made up of fibres twisted together.

c) Fibres are obtained from many sources, natural and chemical.

There are so many fibres today and so many different types of fabric that there is a tendency to confuse the names of the fabrics with the names of the fibres from which they are made, for example nylon is NOT a fabric but a fibre from which the fabric is made, whereas nylon seersucker IS a fabric — seersucker being the name for a fabric woven in a particular way and nylon being the fibre from which the yarn is made for the weaving.

**Examples of fibres are:**

| *Natural* | *Man-made from natural sources* | *Man-made synthetic* |
|---|---|---|
| Silk | Viscose | Polyamides |
| Wool | Cupro | Polyesters |
| Cotton | Acetate | Acrylics |
| Flax | Triacetate | |

In earlier days only the natural fibres were known and the yarn produced from them was woven or knitted in a variety of ways to make the different fabrics. Each type of fabric so produced had its own name. For instance, to mention only a few; velvet, chiffon, crêpe-de-chine were made from silk yarn; lawn, velveteen, corduroy, piqué were made from cotton yarn; fine linen was made from flax yarn; tweed, worsted and jersey from woollen yarn. In these times the rich wore silks, high quality woollens and fine linen, while the poor had to be content with cotton and inferior woollens. However, today we are able to produce fibres from processed natural sources and from chemicals. This is very necessary as there would not be enough of the natural fibres to go round such an increased population as we now have. When man-made fibres first became available, the yarns made from them were used to produce the same types of fabric as had hitherto been made from the natural yarns. It then became necessary to identify the yarn from which a fabric was made because the man-made fibres react differently to sewing and cleaning and behave differently in use from the natural ones. Since 1973 it has been law that all fabrics should be labelled with the fibre content and if more than one fibre has been used in making the fabric the percentages must be given, e.g. 50% polyester 50% cotton. Even if four or five types of fibre are used ALL the percentages must be given.

When buying fabrics by the metre make a note of the fibre content, which is usually to be found on the end of the roller or bale, because only rarely is one given a leaflet containing this information. Knowing the fibre content is important for the following reasons:

a) *Suitability for purpose.*

Silk, wool and bulked man-made yarns are warm to wear; cotton, linen and man-made yarns which have not been treated are cool. Cotton, wool, silk and viscose are absorbent of moisture while polyamides, polyesters and treated woollens are water-repellent.

b) *Easy care.*

Wool is naturally crease-shedding and although its elasticity can cause it to stretch in wear at elbows, knees and the seat, this can usually be pressed out with a damp cloth. Polyamides and polyesters are crease-resistant and also resistant to soiling. Linen and cotton crease badly unless treated. Most man-made fibres are mothproof and are not liable to mildew.

c) *Safety.*

Cotton fabrics are highly inflammable unless treated. Polyamides melt with heat. Some modified viscose yarns such as Durel are flame-retardant.

d) *Laundering and dry-cleaning.*

Wool, cotton, linen and viscose may shrink when washed unless they have a shrink-resist finish. Some man-made fibres are damaged by certain dry-cleaning agents, e.g. acetate will dissolve in nail varnish remover.

Wool will 'felt' if soap is not properly rinsed out and if too much moist heat is applied. Polyamides will melt if the iron is too hot.

Viscose and acetate yarns are weaker when they are wet and should not be rubbed vigorously when washed.

Polyamides and polyesters, being non-absorbent, are quick to dry and can be drip-dried, when the weight of the water running off them will straighten out any creases, thus minimising the need for ironing.

A knowledge of the properties of the various fibres will assist in the correct choice of fabric for each purpose.

Fibres can conveniently be divided into two main groups: those which are produced naturally and those which are man-made. The natural fibres will be considered first and may be shown as follows:

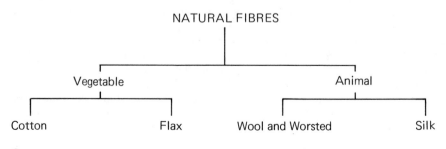

NATURAL FIBRES

Vegetable          Animal

Cotton      Flax      Wool and Worsted      Silk

## COTTON

Cotton fibre is more widely used than other fibres because it is easy to handle, comparatively inexpensive, strong and hardwearing and suitable for many purposes. For example it is used to make bed linen, towels, table linen, curtains, upholstery, clothing of all kinds including heavy industrial overalls and for sewing and embroidery threads.

**The Raw Materials**

Cotton fibres come from a bushy plant which grows in tropical parts of the world, the West Indies, Egypt, Africa, parts of North and South America and India.

Cotton Growing Areas

The seeds of the plant are sown in the spring and the shoots appear in about fourteen days and later they are thinned out in rows. The bushes grow from 1 - 1½ m and in two months they each bear about twenty beautiful flowers. The flowers live for three days only and when they die away they leave behind small green pods each containing thirty to forty seeds. The pods are called bolls and as they ripen the seeds inside become completely covered with fine cotton fibres. These fibres go on growing for about two months until finally they burst the boll and become a fluffy mass like a ball of cotton wool.

The fibres in each boll are of different lengths, some being 2-5 cm long while others are shorter and downy. It is at this stage that they are gathered, by hand or machinery, and as they do not all ripen at the same time they are gathered at intervals of about ten days. Hand picking is best because machines cannot tell the difference between ripe and unripe bolls and so mix and entangle them with leaves and stalks.

Cotton Boll

After they are picked the bolls are fed into machines called *gins* which separate the seeds and some of the stalks and leaves from the cotton fibres. At the same time they separate out the short downy fibres which are too short for making cotton yarn. These short fibres are called cotton lint and are used for making rayon materials.

To make it easy to handle after it has been ginned the cotton is pressed by machinery into tight bales each weighing 240 kg and is then exported as raw cotton to cotton mills all over the world.

### Making the Cotton Fibres into Yarn

When the raw cotton bales arrive at the mills they still contain some seed, grit leaves and bits of stalk and the cotton has been so pressed down in the bales that it has become caked into lumps. The impurities have to be removed and the lumps loosened up before the cotton can be spun. Sometimes the bales are not all of the same quality although they come from the same place so they are mixed together to make them uniform.

### Opening and Breaking

The cotton bales are opened out and broken up in a series of machines which have rollers and beaters fitted with spikes. As the cotton moves along them the rollers comb and tease the fibres tearing them into small pieces and breaking up the lumps. Suction pipes move the bits of cotton along and currents of air blow through to fluff them out and most of the loosened impurities fall through grids in the machines. This beating and fluffing out makes the cotton much more bulky, up to twenty times the size it was when it went into the machines, and it comes out of them in long soft sheets of cotton called *laps* and looks rather like outsize cotton wool as one buys it from the chemist.

## Scutching

The laps of cotton are next passed through a machine called a *scutcher* which contains a revolving beater with two or three blades, fixed over a grid. The cotton passes under the beater which loosens it still further and beats out more impurities, making them fall through the grid.

## Carding

The cotton laps are now fed through the *carding machine* which has revolving cylinders covered all over with fine wires. As the cotton passes through the wire points it is pulled out into a soft rope and the fibres are brushed to lie all in the same direction, parallel with each other. The last impurities are removed and at the end of this machine the cotton is passed through a *comb* which stretches it into a thin loose rope called a *sliver*. As they pass out of the machine the slivers are coiled round into metal cans.

## Drawing

Six slivers at a time are fed out of their cans into another machine, called a *draw frame*, which twists them together and pulls and draws them out into one single, stronger sliver of the same thickness as each of the original six.

## Combing

If the cotton is to be used for making fine material it is combed at this stage by fine needles in a machine to remove any short fibres which would make the yarn fluffy and also to stroke the fibres parallel with each other. Cotton which is to be used for coarser material is not combed.

## Drafting or Roving

The slivers are put into yet another machine which mixes six together again and twists and stretches them out, making them thinner still and finally winding them on bobbins. The slivers are now called *rovings*. Next they go through two more similar machines, but in these only two rovings are twisted together into one. Each machine makes the rovings thinner and thinner until the last one pulls them out to the thickness of coarse string. They have now reached the stage at which they can be spun into yarn.

## Spinning

When the rovings are spun they are twisted together to give them strength and are then drawn out to the required degree of fineness. There are three methods of spinning:

a) *Ring spinning.* In this method the bobbins of rovings are placed on the top of a spinning machine and are drawn downwards through rollers which stretch and twist the yarn and wind it on revolving spindles at the bottom of the machine.

b) *Mule spinning.* This is a slower method used for fine materials. The principle is the same but it is carried out in three separate operations. (1) The yarn is stretched and then (2) it is twisted and finally (3) it is wound on the spindles.

c) *Open-end or Break spinning.* From ancient times it has been the custom to spin yarn by twisting fibres together so that they will cling to each other. The twist is inserted by rotating a bobbin and winding the yarn onto it.. The same principle applies to both mule and ring spinning. As a bobbin will hold only a certain amount of yarn it becomes necessary to replace it with a fresh one as soon as it becomes full. This is time-wasting and a method has now been devised by which the fibres themselves are twisted without using a bobbin. Separate fibres are fed from a drafting machine into an open-ended pot which spins round very rapidly causing the fibres to be flung by centrifugal force against the inner sides of the pot where they become densely packed. Then the fibres are pulled away from the sides of the rotating pot towards the centre and they twist into yarn. By this method a constant supply of fibres into the pot will produce an endless supply of yarn with greater speed and economy, without the need to change bobbins every so often, as they fill.

During spinning, threads which are going to be used for the weft (threads woven across the material) are wound on to cops that fit into shuttles which pass between the warp threads (those which run lengthwise in the material), backwards and forwards, during the weaving. If the cotton is to be mixed with another fibre, such as wool, the two threads are twisted together during the spinning. The yarn is now ready to be woven or knitted into fabric.

## Characteristics of Cotton Fibres

The quality of the cotton depends on how it is grown and from which part of the world it comes. Long, fine fibres make the best material.

*Sea Island cotton.* This is cotton grown only in the West Indies and the small Sea Islands off the south coast of Carolina. It has fine silky fibres which are long — about 3-5 cm — and it is very strong. High-grade materials are made from it which are quite expensive to buy because only a limited amount of this cotton can be grown on these small islands and it cannot be grown anywhere else.

*Egyptian cotton.* The next best in quality. The fibres are long and materials made from them are fairly expensive.

*American cotton.* The fibres are of medium length and are used to make sateens and cambrics. The cotton is not so strong as Egyptian nor does it have such a good appearance. It is cheaper.

*Indian cotton.* This has the shortest and coarsest fibres of all and it is neither so strong nor of such good quality as the other types.

Cotton fibres are made up of *cellulose,* which is a fibrous substance found in all plants, composed of carbon, hydrogen and oxygen. While the fibres are inside the boll on the plant they are like tiny hollow tubes, their nourishment passing up the hollow through the centre. When the cotton boll bursts the hot sun dries the fibres up and they collapse, becoming flat, like ribbon, and twisted. When a cotton fibre is examined under a microscope, it is seen to twist two or three times to the left and then two or three times to the right alternately. These twists make the cotton yarn very strong. The finer, thinner fibres have more twists to the centimetre than the shorter, coarser ones and so are stronger.

The cellulose making up the cotton contains a greasy substance which gives it an off-white or 'grey' colour and prevents it from absorbing water. This substance must be removed before the cotton material can be dyed or finished, otherwise the material will not take the dye.

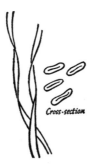

*Cross-section*

Raw Cotton Fibre
Microscopic diagram

**The Properties of Cotton**

1) It is able to absorb moisture up to 40 per cent of its own weight.

2) The absorbed moisture evaporates quickly so the material dries rapidly and this makes cotton cool to wear. For this reason it is a suitable material for underwear, sports clothes, summer clothes and for those worn in hot climates.

3) Some cotton materials are treated to make them fluffy so that air trapped in the fluffiness can make them warmer, e.g. winceyette. Untreated cotton is cool

because the fibres are smooth and do not hold air. Another way to make cotton warmer is to knit it, or to weave it with small spaces between the threads which can hold air. Aertex is an example of the last method.

4) Cotton is a strong fibre which becomes even stronger when wetted. Consequently it can be rubbed, scrubbed and boiled during laundering. It is not harmed by alkalies (soaps and soda), or by heat, or by bleaches if they are used with due care. This means that washing presents no problems and the material is therefore suitable for garments and articles which need frequent laundering. The extra strength when wet makes it particularly suitable for towels.

5) If cotton is left damp in a heap for any length of time, it is attacked by mildew which is difficult to remove without the aid of strong bleaching agents which may weaken the fibres.

6) Cotton is mothproof.

7) Cotton materials in their natural state crease easily but nowadays they can be treated with resin which makes them more crease-resistant.

8) Cotton is inclined to shrink when first washed unless it has been pre-shrunk during manufacture. It is advisable to shrink cotton materials by damping them or immersing them in water before making them up.

9) Long exposure to air, as in the case of curtains, will rot the material.

10) Because it is strong, hardwearing and inexpensive cotton fibre can be mixed with other fibres, such as wool, to reduce the cost and improve the wearing quality.

**Identifying Cotton Material**

One test is to burn a small scrap of the material and if it is cotton it will flare up with a yellow flame and leave behind it only a very little grey ash. This test does not apply when cotton is mixed or blended with another fibre because other fibres react differently to burning.

## LINEN

Linen is the oldest fabric known to man. It was used as long ago as 5000 B.C. and has always been very highly prized. The fibres vary in thickness and can be made into materials of varying thicknesses from heavy fire-fighting hose to the very fine lawn used to make handkerchiefs. Linen fabrics are stronger than cotton and they wear well and last a long time. For example, the fine linen wrapped round ancient Egyptian mummies survives to this day, thousands of years after it was made.

**Characteristics of Flax Fibres**

The fibre used to make linen is flax. Like cotton it is made up of pure cellulose (carbon, hydrogen, oxygen) but it does not contain quite so much because it is difficult to separate out all the impurities. Whereas cotton fibres come from the seeds of cotton bushes, flax fibres are found in the stalks of the flax plant.

If the stalk is cut across and examined under a microscope it can be seen that the centre is made up of pith surrounded by a woody part round which the bundles of fibres are arranged inside the outer covering. The fibres are smooth round tubes with a hollow running down the centre of each and, at intervals, they have joints like bamboo canes. They have no elasticity and can be split both downwards and across.

Section Across Flax Stem

The bundles of fibres are short, 2½-4 cm in length, but as each bundle slightly overlaps the next down the whole length of the stalk from the tip to the root, they can be kept together in longer lengths. The joints in the fibres also help to make them cling together down the length of the stem and this is further assisted by a gummy substance called pectin. For this reason, when the plants are harvested, they are pulled up by the roots so that none of the fibre shall be wasted or damaged as would be the case if they were cut down. It is important to keep the fibre bundles together in long lengths because they will then make high-grade materials. The overlapping of the bundles causes the yarn made from flax to be of an uneven thickness as a rule. When the fibres are wet, they swell and become stronger and this is why flax is so suitable for making fishing nets and also why linen materials make good towels.

(Linen) Flax Fibre
Microscopic diagram

## The Raw Material

The flax plant grows well in various temperatures but hot tropical climates are unsuitable. The best quality flax is grown in Holland, Belgium, France and Russia. Northern Ireland produces good flax, but the quality varies with the weather at harvesting time. Attempts have been made to grow it in England but these have not prospered greatly. Russia grows far more than all the other countries put together.

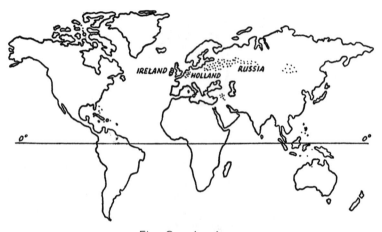

Flax Growing Areas

Each year the tiny seeds are sown in the spring very thickly so that they will grow up tall to reach the light and in doing so help to keep each other straight. The slender plants grow to about one metre in height and they bear very pretty flowers which may be either blue or white. The blue variety produces the finest fibres.

Linseed oil is obtained from the seeds of flax plants which are grown especially for this purpose. The fibres in the stems of such plants are used for 'tow' which will be explained later. When the plants are grown to produce fibre for linen, they are harvested in the autumn just before the seeds are fully ripe as the fibre is at its best at this stage. The harvesting is best carried out by hand but nowadays machines are used to pull the plants up by the roots. The plants are left in small stacks to dry out, after which they have to go through several processes before the fibre is ready for use.

## Rippling

The stalks are combed by spikes called ripples, to remove the leaves and seeds. In former days this used to be done by hand.

## Retting

The flax fibres have to be separated from those parts of the plant which are not wanted, such as the outer covering, and the inner woody part and the pith.

The longest fibres make the best quality linen but, as has been mentioned previously, the fibres are naturally short and held together by pectin in longer lengths of up to one metre. Therefore it is important when separating them out to keep them together in the longest lengths possible. This is done by rotting away some of the unwanted parts of the plant, leaving the fibres intact, and may be carried out by one of three methods:—

*a)* The plants are stacked into sheaves and left exposed to the weather and dew for several weeks, or

*b)* they are left lying in rivers or stagnant pools, or

*c)* they are left in special tanks where the temperature of the water is kept even.

Whichever method is used the result is the same. Bacteria attack the stems, rotting the fleshy parts and loosening the fibres so that they can be separated easily. This process requires very careful timing, because if it is carried out for too long, the fibres themselves begin to rot.

## Scutching

The next stage is carried out by machinery. The flax is dried and passed through pairs of rollers, which are fluted, to break down the woody parts of the stalks without damaging the fibres. The revolving wooden beaters of the scutching machine clean out the broken-down impurities and separate and comb the flax fibres into greyish-brown or flaxen-coloured hanks which are ready for spinning into yarn.

## Spinning

The first process is called *hackling*. The flax is prepared for spinning by being mechanically combed out through sets of pins in a hackling machine to straighten the fibres and make them all lie in the same direction. The long fibres are known as 'flax lines' and the combing process removes all the loose short ones which are called 'tow'. Flax tow is used for making twine and materials of not such good quality as the flax line makes.

After hackling, the fibres are formed into slivers which go through drawing processes like cotton, to put a twist into them for extra strength and to draw them out to the required degree of fineness, ready for making into material. At this stage the yarn is unbleached and is known as 'grey yarn'. The weaver boils or bleaches it to get it as white as possible so that it will take dye. Only mild bleaches can be used as acids harm the fibres.

Apart from making it into materials, flax is used for button thread and embroidery threads because it is so strong and lasts so long.

**The Properties of Linen**

1) Linen is stronger than cotton, but as it is not twisted like cotton it is not at all elastic. This makes it suitable for hose pipes and fishing nets, both needing a strong fibre which will not stretch.

2) As the fibres are not elastic they will split, both across and lengthwise if treated badly during laundering. This is a disadvantage in the case of table linen because, if, after washing, folds are repeatedly ironed in the same places, the fibres will eventually crack and split along the folds.

3) Linen creases easily, but it can be made crease-resistant if treated with resin.

4) Linen materials absorb a little more moisture than cotton and this evaporates quickly making them cool to wear, therefore they are suitable for summer dresses and suits and for bed linen.

5) The fibres are smooth and in no way fluffy and this gives material made from them a natural sheen which is attractive, particularly in table linen. The smoothness prevents the materials picking up dirt so they stay clean a long time. The non-fluffiness and absorbency of linen makes it especially good for tea towels, glass cloths and handkerchiefs.

6) As the short fibres overlap to make longer lengths, the yarn is usually of uneven thickness giving an uneven texture to materials. However, linen can be made from fibres of even thickness and is known as *even weave linen*. This is usually expensive on account of the quality, but is essential for counted thread embroidery to obtain stitches of an even size.

7) Like cotton, if linen is left damp in a heap for a time it is attacked by mildew which is difficult to remove.

8) The effects of acids and alkalies on linen are the same as for cotton.

**Identifying Linen**

Linen flares up and burns with a yellow flame just like cotton and leaves behind a grey ash.

## WOOL

Wool has been used as a fibre for making cloth since prehistoric times. It has very special qualities which no other fibres possess, although many attempts have been made to imitate it. The fibres are obtained from sheep, alpaca goats, rabbits and other furry animals, but it is the sheep's wool that we use more than any other. The main producing countries are Australia, New Zealand, South Africa, U.S.A., Argentina, Uraguay and Russia. The best type of wool is merino wool and is very soft and fine. It comes from merino sheep, originally a Spanish breed. India also produces wool but it is coarse and suitable only for making carpets.

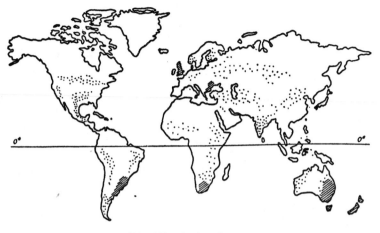

Wool Producing Areas

### The Properties of Wool Fibres

1) Wool is a protein fibre containing keratin, a protein made of several amino-acids. Amino-acids are the substances which make up proteins. The fibres have an inner part or core enclosed in an outer skin which is made up of small irregular, overlapping scales. These scales are very important as they play a big part in giving warmth and felting properties to wool fibres. The quality of the fibres varies according to the part of the fleece from which they come. They may be from 4-40 cm long and it is the long fine fibres which make the best quality materials.

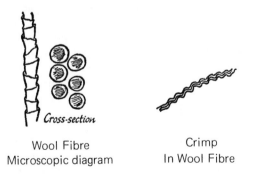

Wool Fibre
Microscopic diagram

Crimp
In Wool Fibre

2) Wool fibres are crimped. That is to say, they are very wavy (see diagram) and the finer fibres have more crimps in them than the coarse ones. If the fibres

are pulled out straight and then let go they will always spring back in crimps to their original length. This makes materials woven or knitted from woollen yarn very elastic and garments made from them are comfortable to wear because they will stretch and give with the movements of the body so that one does not feel restricted in them. Admittedly, with repeated stretching and strain, tight woollen skirts will 'seat' and trousers will 'bag' at the knees, but the fibres are so elastic that if they are pressed under a damp cloth with a warm iron they will spring back to their former size and the 'bagginess' will disappear. During the processes through which the fibres have to go to be made into yarn and then into fabric, they do become somewhat stretched so that when the material is washed or cleaned, they spring back to their original length and cause shrinking. Today, woollen fabrics are often pre-shrunk or treated with shrink-resistant chemicals by the manufacturers before they reach the shops. However, when buying woollen materials which are not guaranteed pre-shrunk it is wise to shrink them by wrapping in a damp cloth or by damp pressing, before cutting out and making up garments from them.

3) Wool fibres have the unique property of being able to absorb moisture without feeling wet. They can take up as much as 30 per cent of their own weight in moisture before becoming damp and uncomfortable so that a coat weighing 1½ kg can contain about half a litre of water and not feel damp. The curious thing about this, which scientists still do not understand, is that, as it absorbs this water vapour the wool gains extra warmth. For this reason it makes ideal materials to wear next to the skin in winter and to put on after playing strenuous games, because the fibres will absorb perspiration, give out warmth and prevent one from feeling chilly. It is also particularly suitable for overcoats, for when the surrounding air is charged with moisture the fibres absorb it and then produce extra heat to keep the body warm.

This absorbency makes it necessary to dry woollen garments thoroughly after washing them. In fact, they should be aired for twenty-four hours and, even then, it is not possible to air the moisture out of them completely.

4) Because it absorbs vapour so well it seems rather strange that wool should also have the power of repelling water, but this is so. Drops of rain will stay on the fluffy surface of a woollen coat for some time, before they penetrate the cloth, and can be shaken off quite easily.

5) Apart from the heat produced when the fibres are damp there is another more important way in which they give warmth. This is brought about by the overlapping scales wrapped round the fibres which project a little, holding the fibres slightly away from each other so that pockets of air are trapped between them. Therefore wool is a bad conductor of heat because it keeps warmth in the body.

6) If wool fibres are rubbed and pressed together and heated when they are wet, the projecting scales become entangled with each other and interlock so that they can no longer be separated. This causes woollen garments which are roughly washed or rubbed in water to felt up. When this happens, the spaces

between the fibres close up and the material becomes dense and thickened and when there are no longer any air spaces, wool loses its warmth; therefore careful laundering is essential.

7) Alkalies are harmful to the fibres and as soap is alkaline all traces should be rinsed out after washing. Soda should not be used, but when it is necessary to soften hard water, which makes the fibres harsh, a milder alkali, such as borax, can be used with care. Diluted acids do not appear to harm the fibres, but they absorb them and this may make it difficult to rinse dirty soap out completely after washing. Strong acid bleaches should not be used at all as they make the fabric harsh and yellowish in colour, but mild bleaches, such as peroxide of hydrogen and potassium permanganate may be used safely.

8) The grubs of the clothes-moth like to feed on wool and can do a great deal of damage. Nowadays fabrics are usually given mothproof treatment.

## Making the Fibres into Yarn

The wool is sheared from the sheep and sorted out for quality. Then it is packed into bales weighing about 140 kg each and sent to the mills. On arrival at the mills the wool is dirty, for it contains dried perspiration, natural oil, to which dirt sticks, and many impurities which the sheep pick up from the land. It has to be cleaned, and this is done by washing it several times in soapy water, after which it is well rinsed. Then any solid impurities clinging to the fibres are removed, and they are ready to be made into one of two different types of yarn, as very briefly outlined below.

*Woollen yarn.* For this the shorter fibres are used to make yarn for weaving into hairy types of material.

*a)* The fibres are treated with oil to help them withstand the various processes through which they have to go.

*b)* They are carded by being passed between pairs of rollers covered with fine wires which comb them to lie in different directions to produce the hairy effect. They come out of the carding machine in a very fine film of wool.

*c)* The layer of wool is divided up into slivers which are doubled (mixed together) and drafted out into thinner rovings ready for spinning.

*d)* The rovings are spun by being twisted together and drafted out until they are fine enough for weaving.

*Worsted yarn.* The longer fibres are used to make a yarn for good quality smooth fabrics.

*a)* The fibres are combed by machinery to make them all lie parallel with each other and so produce a smooth yarn.

*b)* The slivers are put into a *gilling machine* in which they pass between revolving rollers to be drawn out thin enough for winding into balls.

*c)* The oil is washed off the slivers and they are dried.

*d)* Then they are combed again to keep them parallel and to remove any short ones which would make the yarn fluffy.

*e)* Six slivers are fed into a machine which mixes them together and draws them out into a thin single roving ready for spinning.

*Regenerated and virgin wool.* Not all wool is new. It is possible to reduce worn-out woollen garments to wool fibres again, and this is why they are so sought after by rag merchants. The old wool is cleaned and shredded back into wool fibres which are then spun again into yarn. This regenerated wool is perfectly good but naturally it does not have such a long life as new wool. Sometimes it is mixed with new fibres to improve the yarn. Because a garment is labelled 'All Wool' it does not necessarily mean that it is all new wool, it may be a mixture of old and new and the label will still be correct. Only when it is labelled Pure New Wool is a garment made entirely from new wool.

*The Woolmark.* This is an International Symbol used by manufacturers of made-up articles who have been licensed to use it by the International Wool Secretariat Nominee Co. Ltd. It is used in 90 countries and denotes that an article is made from pure new wool allowing for a maximum of 5% non-wool fibre which may have been used to give a decorative effect and 0.3% for accidental impurities. These standards are being constantly checked. See diagram.

The Woolmark

*The Woolblendmark.* This is used when pure wool is blended with another fibre or when this blended fibre is used in making up parts of pure woollen garments, e.g. heels and toes of socks. See diagram.

The Woolblendmark

*Scottish Woollen Publicity Council's Trade Mark.* Cloth woven in Scotland bears St. Andrew's Cross and a Thistle beside the woolmark. See diagram.

Scottish Woollen Publicity
Council's Trade Mark

*Superwash wool.* This is wool which can be machine washed. It is treated with a small amount of resin. Such wool has a special label which may incorporate either the woolmark or the woolblendmark, as in the diagram.

Superwash Wool

For worsted fabrics the treatment can be applied to the yarn before the fabric is made. In the case of knitted goods it can be added afterwards when they are made up. This treatment will neither wash nor wear out and the fibres are actually strengthened by the process.

## Identifying Wool

Wool is not inflammable and if a scrap is burnt it will only smoulder and then go into a black bead smelling strongly of burnt hair, which is what it really is. Its appearance under a microscope is very characteristic as mentioned before.

## SILK

Silk threads were used to make lovely material as long ago as 2500 B.C. by the Chinese, who guarded the secret so closely that it did not reach Europe until about A.D. 600. Today silk is produced in Japan, China, India, Italy, France and Asia Minor. Japan is the largest exporting country.

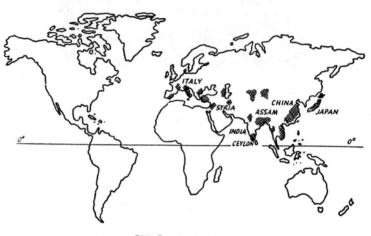

Silk Producing Areas

### The Raw Material

The silk fibres are obtained from the caterpillar of a spinning moth. Some of these moths are wild and the materials made from them are called 'wild silks', Tussore being one of the best known. The cultivated moth, from which the best quality silk comes, is the species *Bombyx mori*.

Each moth lays up to 400 eggs in the summer and, as they are subject to disease, they have to be examined and carefully selected. They are very, very tiny and so are the grubs which hatch out of them. These minute silkworms live on mulberry leaves of which they eat such an enormous amount that by the end of about five weeks they have become 7½ cm long, having, in the meantime, shed their coats four times as they outgrew them. After this the caterpillar gets restless and seeks some secluded twig on which to fix its cocoon. Inside the .silkworm are two glands running down the whole length of its body, each having an opening close to the mouth. The glands produce a sticky protein fluid called *fibroin,* made up of carbon, oxygen, hydrogen and nitrogen. When the fibroin comes in contact with air, it dries and forms the silken thread. At the same time the silkworm produces, from two other glands, a gummy substance called *sericin,* or silk-gum, which sticks the two fibroin threads together so that they emerge as one single thread from an opening just under the mouth. The silkworm fixes this thread to a twig and then, with circular movements of its head, winds the silk round and round its body for two days and nights until it is enclosed completely within an oval silken shell, which is usually yellow or white. The sericin sets in the air, binding the silk together and making the shell firm. Altogether the silkworm spins and winds round itself approximately three kilometres of silk thread and it winds it round from within, in such a way that one end of the cocoon is a little thinner than the rest of it. Inside the cocoon the silkworm turns into a chrysalis which in turn becomes the moth. Now when the moth is ready to come out of the cocoon, it produces a solution to soften the thin end so that it can bore its way through into the outside world. When it does this it spoils the silk by breaking it so that it cannot be wound off into the long lengths which are required to make high-grade materials. Therefore, when the cocoon is wanted for silk, the chrysalis is killed, by steam or hot air, before it is ready to emerge, so that the silk can be wound off in a continuous length. Of course, some of the moths are allowed to develop normally for breeding purposes, otherwise silkworms would die out. The cocoons of these are used for waste silk which will be described later.

## Making the Silk into Yarn

### Reeling

The unwinding of the silk is known as reeling. The thread cannot be unwound until the silk-gum holding it together has been softened. This is done by putting the cocoons into hot water which does no harm to the fibres but melts the gum. Then, by careful and gentle brushing, an end can be found which will unwind. The silk thread is so fine that it cannot be used as it is, therefore the threads from five or seven cocoons are twisted together as they are unwound and

Reeling Silk

the gum, drying again, holds them in a single stronger thread. It is not possible to unwind the entire cocoon without the thread breaking, in fact, between a quarter and a third only can be unwound before it breaks. These long lengths are called 'raw silk' and the rest of the cocoon is waste silk which is unwound in shorter lengths, to be spun together eventually, in much the same way as cotton fibres, to make yarn for schappe silk and spun silk materials. The raw silk is made into skeins which are sent to the thrower who makes them into yarn.

### Throwing

This is the process of converting raw silk into either one of two types of yarn.
*a) Tram yarn,* in which two or three lengths of raw silk are twisted together loosely. This type of yarn is used for weft threads in woven materials.
*b) Organzine yarn,* which is used for warp threads as it is stronger. The lengths of silk are doubled and twisted and then doubled and twisted again, but this time in the opposite direction, to give extra strength.

When the yarn is loosely twisted, materials made from it have a beautiful soft lustre but when it is tightly twisted some of this lustre is lost. These two yarns are known as *nett silk* and from them high-grade materials are made, which are expensive.

### Spinning

All the waste silk and short fibres are collected together to be made into *spun silk yarn.* This makes quite a different type of material from nett silk. It is usually cheaper to buy. On the Continent spun silk is sometimes known as schappe silk as the word *schappe* in French and German is an exact translation of the English term 'spun silk'.
*a)* The silk-gum is removed by boiling in soapy water and this makes the silk much lighter in weight.
*b)* The threads are dried and, as most of them are different lengths, they are put into a machine which combs them straight and cuts them into uniform lengths of 15 cm.
*c)* Some of the fibres are shorter than 15 cm to begin with and these are now separated out into lengths of 10 cm and 12½ cm. Then any which are shorter than this are separated out again and put on one side to be used for making noil yarn, which is described later.
*d)* The fibres are put into another machine which makes them into a lap 90 cm wide. This lap is then pulled out into slivers which are doubled together and then drafted out to make the fibres lie parallel to each other.
*e)* Eventually the slivers are drafted into rovings ready for spinning. The spinning processes are much the same as those used for cotton. Usually two rovings are spun together to make the yarn for material, and three when sewing thread is

made. These are known as two-fold and three-fold yarns.

*f)* The yarn is passed quickly through a gas flame to singe off any projecting fibres which would make it fluffy.

## Weighting

The amount of gum in silk varies and after it has been degummed during processing, the yarn becomes thinner and lighter in weight so that, in order to give silk materials substance, the yarn is sometimes weighted. This means that a compound of tin or some other metallic salt is introduced into the silk to make it heavier and thicker. Within reason this does no harm, but if too much weighting is added the silk deteriorates quickly and does not wear well.

## Noil

When waste silk is spun there is still further waste in the fibres which are too short to be used for spun silk. These are collected up and carded and spun into coarser yarns, which by this time have lost their lustre. This yarn is used for industrial purposes and can make very good dress material, known as noil, which is remarkably inexpensive and excellent value for money.

## Blended Fibres

Silk can be mixed with other fibres, such as wool, rayon, nylon, to add strength, elasticity and warmth, but pure silk by itself is the most luxurious of all materials and cannot be improved upon. It has no equal.

## Characteristics of Silk

1) Materials made from nett silk have a lovely soft sheen and they are most pleasant to handle. This makes them ideal for luxurious underwear.

2) Silk is a good insulator, warm to wear in the winter and cool in the summer, another reason why it is so suitable for lingerie.

3) It is absorbent and, like wool, acquires extra warmth when slightly damp.

4) Silk is one of the strongest natural fibres.

5) It is very elastic which makes it wear well and for this reason it is most suitable for sewing thread which will 'give' with the material when it is stretched so that seams will not break easily under strain.

6) The elastic quality makes it crease-resistant. Silk materials recover quickly from creasing which shakes out. This makes them particularly useful for garments which have to be packed or worn for travelling.

7) The fact that silk materials weigh so little is an important factor when packing for air travel when baggage weight is limited.

8) Some silk materials will drape beautifully and softly while others are so stiff that they will stand by themselves. Therefore they make lovely bridal and evening dresses.

9) Silk is not harmed by mild acids although the fibres absorb and retain them in the same way that wool does. Ammonia does not hurt the fibres at all but strong acids will destroy them, so that when it is necessary to use bleaches, only mild ones, such as hydrogen peroxide, should be used. Unfortunately the natural colour of silk is difficult to bleach a pure white.

10) Alkalies will make the fibres tender but will not cause so much damage to them as to wool fibres. However, strong caustic solutions will dissolve silk fibres. Tussore, which is a wild silk from India, does not appear to be harmed by alkalies.

11) If too much heat is used when silk materials are washed the fibres become tender and white silk turns yellowish.

12) If silk is rubbed during washing the fibres may break, particularly if the material has been weighted.

13) Weighted materials are rotted by exposure to sunlight and so are best worn indoors.

14) Perspiration will rot silk fabrics and dress shields should be stitched into all silk dresses and blouses.

15) Silk is not so likely to be attacked by moth grubs as wool, that is, if it is clean. However, if silk is dirty, the grubs will eat the dirt and in doing so will damage the fibres.

### Identifying Silk

The threads are smooth and softly lustrous. Under a microscope they look like smooth rods but the cross-section is not round but rather irregular in shape.

Burn a small piece of material and, if it is pure silk, it will smoulder and run into a black bead. If the silk is weighted the metallic salt used for the loading will cause it to glow like red hot metal. Pure silk will smell like burnt feathers but weighted silk may not smell so strongly.

Silk Fibre
Microscopic diagram

Put a scrap of the material into a 5 per cent solution of hot caustic soda and if the material is silk it will dissolve.

When silk is blended with wool fibres both react in the same way to the tests but the texture of the material should be a guide, for no silk is as hairy as wool and no wool as smooth and lustrous as silk. If the silk is mixed with acetate fibres and a scrap of material is soaked in acetone (nail varnish remover) the acetate fibres will dissolve leaving the silk fibres intact.

## MAN-MADE FIBRES

To make these fibres man has borrowed the silk-worm's method, that is, to make a sticky liquid which will solidify into threads in the presence of air or by means of chemicals.

The first man-made fibres were very shiny and were known as 'artificial silk'. Today this name is not used because these fibres have become so important in themselves that they no longer act as a substitute for silk. There are very many of them and the research needed to make a new fibre is very costly. Nowadays for economic reasons research is mainly concentrated on improving such fibres as have already been discovered rather than on producing new fibres. There are several types of man-made fibres and these are shown in the following table:

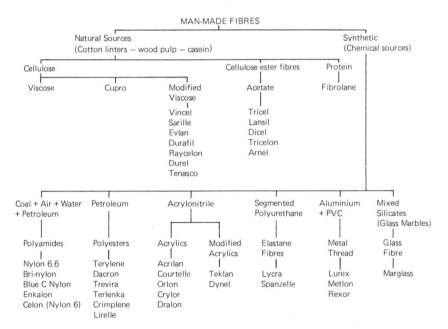

These fibres are made from many substances — wood, cotton linters, casein, coal, petroleum, and so on. The basic substance is made by treating materials with chemicals or by melting to produce a sticky liquid which is forced in fine streams through a spinneret containing from one to several hundred holes. These streams of liquid harden in several ways into fine threads, a number of which are twisted together to form·the yarn. The thickness of yarn can be varied by the number of threads twisted together, by the size of the holes in the spinneret and the speed with which the liquid is forced through. When it is forced through quickly the filaments are thinner than when it is trickled through slowly. Yarn is very regular.

Two kinds of yarn can be made (1) continuous filament yarn and (2) staple yarn.

Spinneret

### Continuous Filament Yarn

Unending streams of filaments are twisted together to make continuous unbroken lustrous yarn which is used for taffetas, satins and materials with a sheen. Dull, matt yarn is made by putting a white pigment into the liquid before spinning.

Filament          Staple

## Staple Yarn

This starts as a thick tow — a much thicker filament yarn. It is then cut or broken by stretching into short lengths which are mixed together and spun in the ways that cotton, linen and wool are spun and the whole character of the yarn is changed. The projecting ends of the innumerable short fibres produce a dull yarn which can be used to make many types of fabrics.

The rope-like tow is cut up as it is made and the short lengths are called staple fibre. The fibre is then washed, purified and dried in hot air in special ovens, after which it is packed into bales and sent to the spinning mills.

Man-made fibres can be divided into two main classes, (a) those which are derived from natural sources, e.g. cellulose and (b) those which are chemically made from mineral sources.

Fibres from natural sources used to be called Rayon, but this name is being dropped in favour of Viscose and Acetate.

## VISCOSE

The flow chart overleaf shows how Courtaulds' Viscose is made.

### The Properties of Viscose

*a)* In all man-made fibres colour can be put into the spinning solution before this is made into filaments. This is useful because fabric made from coloured yarn does not require dyeing and the colour remains fast, right through the material.
*b)* Viscose absorbs moisture and is a good conductor of heat.
*c)* Viscose materials are soft to handle and drape well.
*d)* Materials are mothproof and not subject to mildew.
*e)* A point to remember when washing is that hard wringing may cause damage, as the fibre is slightly weaker when wet. Follow the instructions on the care label, remembering that any light-weight fabric should be treated with care. Alkalies do not harm the fibres but acids weaken them.
*f)* The yarn is fairly strong and can be made into many different kinds of fabrics suitable for clothing, household furnishings and for industrial purposes.

### Identifying Viscose

When viscose is set alight it will burn and leave a grey ash, but, of course, this does not apply if the yarn is mixed with another fibre.

Under a microscope the yarn looks like glass rods streaked with parallel or wavy lines.

*Cross-section*

Viscose Fibre Microscopic diagram

Viscose Manufacture

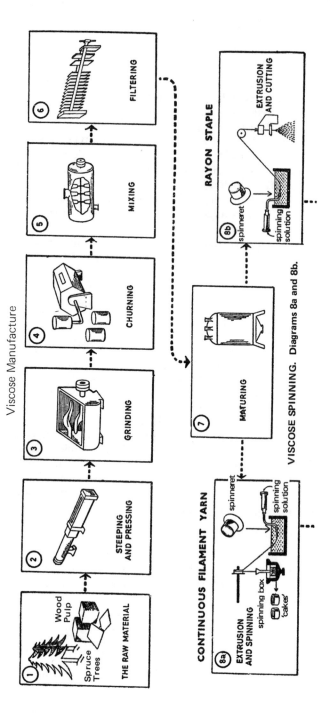

**CONTINUOUS FILAMENT YARN**

**RAYON STAPLE**

**VISCOSE SPINNING. Diagrams 8a and 8b.**

1. THE RAW MATERIAL — Spruce Trees, Wood Pulp
2. STEEPING AND PRESSING
3. GRINDING
4. CHURNING
5. MIXING
6. FILTERING
7. MATURING
8a. EXTRUSION AND SPINNING — spinneret, spinning solution, spinning box, 'cakes'
8b. EXTRUSION AND CUTTING — spinneret, spinning solution

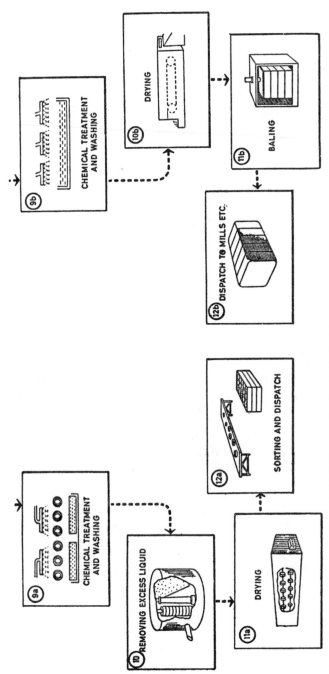

*Reproduced by courtesy of the British Man-made Fibres Federation*

## MODIFIED VISCOSE

This yarn is similar to standard Viscose from the care point of view but the physical properties are modified during manufacture to give the fibres different aesthetic characteristics or to make them suitable for uses which require them to behave differently from standard viscose. The following are examples of modified viscose:

**a) Sarille**

A crimped viscose yarn in staple form with the following properties:

1) It is strong.
2) It resists abrasion.
3) It has a permanent built-in crimp which prevents the fibres packing closely together in a yarn, thus producing bulkiness and a soft warm handle.
4) It has a little tendency to crease.

It is very suitable for between-seasons apparel. Bush baby type fabrics are made from it for children's dresses. It is also used to make tufted and candlewick fabrics and blankets.

**b) Durel**

Viscose modified to be flame-retardant.

**c) Tenasco (High tenacity fibre)**

This is a modified filament yarn which has high strength and resistance to abrasion. It is used for sewing threads, upholstery and safety belts.

**d) Vincel (Modal fibre)**

This staple fibre is one of the modified viscose fibres which is more difficult to stretch when it is wet than the standard viscose.

The physical properties of Vincel are more like cotton than are those of any other man-made fibre.

1) It does not shrink progressively with repeated washing as some rayon fibres do.
2) It is firmer and crisper than standard viscose.
3) It has a lustre similar to mercerised cotton.
4) It washes and wears well.
5) It absorbs slightly more moisture than cotton.

Vincel is used to produce knitted fabrics for underwear, cardigans, dresses and sportswear. It can be used alone or blended with other man-made or natural fibres for making woven fabrics for dresses, lingerie, slacks and shirtings.

Knitted underwear can be washed in hot water or boiled. Other garments should be washed in warm water and ironed slightly damp, using a medium hot iron.

## CUPRO

This yarn is made mainly in Italy. It is made from a solution of copper and ammonia and the copper causes it to become a bright blue colour.

*a)* Cotton linters are put into the solution and they dissolve.

*b)* After it has been filtered, this solution is forced through the spinneret into a tank of water which solidifies the thread.

*c)* The filaments are stretched until they are very fine, but owing to the cuprammonium solution, they are a bright blue. Therefore the yarn is wound into hanks which are put into weak sulphuric acid to wash out the copper and with it, the colour.

This yarn is very fine and smooth and closely resembles silk, for which it is sometimes used as a substitute. As it is made from cotton cellulose, alkalies do it no harm but acids cause deterioration. Like viscose yarn it is weak when it is wet.

Cuprammonium Fibre
Microscopic diagram

## ACETATE

This fibre used to be made from cotton linters (waste cotton fibres too short for spinning into cotton yarn) as shown in the flow chart. Nowadays it is made from wood pulp — both cotton and wood consist of pure cellulose.

*a)* This cellulose is steeped in a solution of acetic acid, acetic anhydride and a catalyst (which may be sulphuric acid) and is converted into cellulose triacetate.

*b)* A little water is added, the solution left to ripen, and the triacetate changes to acetate.

*c)* The sediment is dried out and becomes a white flaky powder.

*d)* The powder is mixed with acetone which dissolves it and combines with it to form the viscous solution for spinning. (Wet spinning)

*e)* The solution is filtered to remove any flakes which may not have dissolved.

*f)* Then it is forced through the spinneret into a current of warm air which evaporates the acetone and solidifies the filaments.

*g)* The filaments are twisted together into continuous filament yarn or the yarn is cut up into staple lengths ready for spinning.

### The Properties of Acetate Materials

*a)* They absorb moisture and are good conductors of heat.

*b)* They may have either lustrous or matt surfaces and have a rich appearance.

Acetate Manufacture

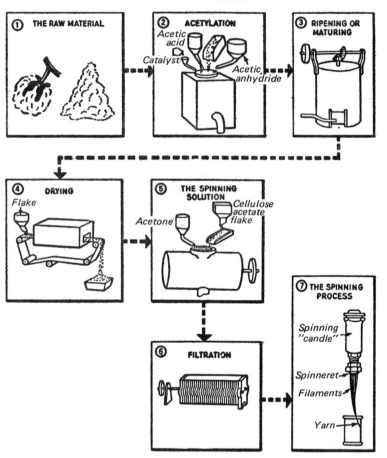

Reproduced by courtesy of the British
Man made Fibres Federation

*c)* They drape softly.

*d)* They neither shrink nor stretch.

*e)* They recover quickly from creasing when they are dry, but care should be taken to crease them as little as possible when they are wet as creases ironed in when the material is damp may be difficult to remove.

*f)* They take dye well and the colour may be introduced in the spinning solution and remains fast. Acetates can be dyed to a wide range of bright colours.

*g)* They last a long time and age does not rot them.

*h)* They are not attacked by moths or mildew.

*i)* They will wash easily provided they are not allowed to become too dirty.

*j)* Too much heat will cause the fibres to melt and fuse together into a black brittle mass. Therefore the heat of the iron during laundering should be very moderate. These materials must never be damped down for ironing because the uneven dampness makes permanent watermarks.

*k)* Acetate is not harmed by most dry cleaning chemicals of the petrol type, but on no account should acetone be used as this is the solution in which the cotton linters were dissolved to make the spinning liquid and it will dissolve them again. When garments made from acetate are sent for dry cleaning they should be labelled clearly that they are acetate. Care should be taken not to spill nail varnish remover on to them, as this also is acetone. Trichlorethylene is also harmful.

*l)* The fibres are naturally very white and do not require bleaching before dyeing. This whiteness is permanent and does not yellow with age.

*m)* Strong alkalies damage the fibre and destroy the lustre. Dilute acids may be used safely provided they are washed out thoroughly afterwards.

Acetate Fibre
Microscopic diagram

**Identifying Acetate**

*a)* Burn a scrap and it should flare up, melt into a black bead and give off an acrid smell.

*b)* Put a scrap into acetone and it will dissolve.

**Dicel**

An acetate yarn in filament form also made by British Celanese Ltd. It can be made bright or dull depending on the purpose for which it is to be used. Fabrics made from it drape very well and have a soft handle making them suitable for dresses, evening wear, lingerie, linings and trimmings.

## TRIACETATE

This is a development of acetate and the yarn is made by various firms. Courtaulds make this yarn under the name of Tricel and another yarn called Arnel is made in the U.S.A. and Luxembourg.

This yarn is made from wood pulp treated with acetic acid, acetic anhydride and a catalyst to make a viscous solution of cellulose triacetate. Water is added and the sediment is dried out. However, the dried triacetate flakes do not dissolve in acetone and are usually put into a solution of methylene chloride to form the spinning fluid. The filaments solidify in warm air.

### The Properties of Triacetate Material

The properties are much the same as those of acetate with the following additions:

*a)* It is less absorbent than acetate and therefore dries quickly.
*b)* Triacetate can be dyed to a wide range of colours.
*c)* It does not pick up dirt easily and stays clean longer than many other materials.
*d)* It resists heat and will be safe in hot water, although for colour fastness and to avoid creasing, it is best washed in water at 40°C, and any soiling comes out easily.
*e)* If drip-dried, it needs very little ironing. When ironing is necessary a warm iron can be used and a steam iron gives the best results.
*f)* It washes and wears well.
*g)* It can be permanently embossed and set into permanent pleats with heat. It is often mixed with other fibres for this reason.
*h)* It dry-cleans safely in white spirit or perchlorethylene. Trichlorethylene damages it.

### Identifying Triacetate

*a)* If burnt it runs away from the flame into a bead.
*b)* If steeped in methylene chloride it will dissolve.

## PROTEIN FIBRES

Fibres can be made from casein, which is a protein in milk. Fibrolane is one. It is a staple fibre and is often blended with wool and some man-made fibres. It has a soft warm handle, and is used for furnishing fabrics.

## SYNTHETIC FIBRES

### POLYAMIDE FIBRES *(Nylon)*

Nylon was the first fibre to be made entirely from chemicals, originally in the U.S.A. There are several forms of nylon, such as nylon 6.6, mainly produced as Bri-nylon by ICI in the Commonwealth, Europe and the U.S.A., and as Blue C nylon by Monsanto Textiles in Luxembourg. Nylon 6 (originally developed in Germany, using the same materials but different chemical processes) is produced as Celon by Courtaulds and Enkalon by British Enkalon.

*How nylon is made*

*a)* Benzene or phenol (chemicals obtained from coal tar), oxygen and nitrogen, obtained from air, and hydrogen, obtained from water, are the basic substances which go to make up nylon. They are combined together to form two chemicals called adipic acid and hexamethylene diamine for Nylon 6.6 and Caprolactam for Nylon 6.

*b)* The chemicals are heated together to form a hot syrupy liquid called a polyamide.

*c)* This hot polymer liquid is poured over a revolving roller while cold water is sprayed on to it. As it cools it turns into a solid white strip which looks rather like marble and which is called a polymer.

*d)* The polymer is cut up into flakes called polymer chips.

*e)* These chips are fed into a machine which heats them so that they melt into a spinning liquid. (Melt spinning)

*f)* As the chips melt the liquid is forced through the spinneret into a current of air to cool and solidify the filaments which are then wound together on cylinders.

*g)* The yarn goes through a cold drawing process in which it is stretched out to four times its original length. This makes it very fine and strong and elastic.

### Nylon Staple

A 'tow' is made from a great number of filaments. It is stretched and crimped and then cut into staple lengths ready for spinning into yarn.

### Properties

*a)* Nylon material is very fine, extremely strong, elastic and light in weight.

*b)* It does not absorb moisture and therefore can be drip-dried very quickly because the moisture runs off.

*c)* It is not weakened when it is wet.

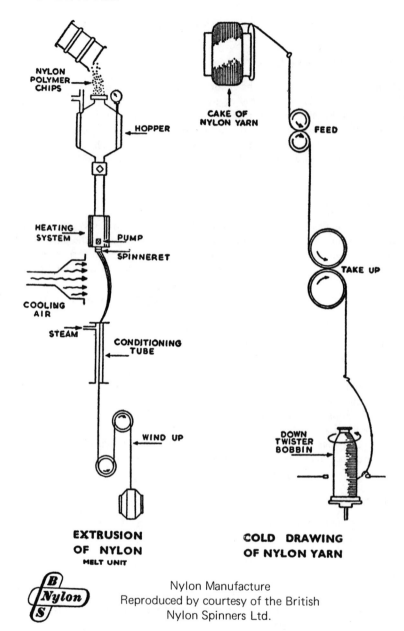

NYLON POLYMER CHIPS

HOPPER

HEATING SYSTEM

PUMP

SPINNERET

COOLING AIR

STEAM

CONDITIONING TUBE

WIND UP

**EXTRUSION OF NYLON**
MELT UNIT

CAKE OF NYLON YARN

FEED

TAKE UP

DOWN TWISTER BOBBIN

**COLD DRAWING OF NYLON YARN**

Nylon Manufacture
Reproduced by courtesy of the British
Nylon Spinners Ltd.

*d)* It is not affected by alkalies or weak acids, but bleaches are harmful.

*e)* It can be dry-cleaned safely with benzene, carbon tetrachloride and trichlorethylene. If nylon articles are sent for dry-cleaning they should be clearly labelled nylon because certain solvents dissolve or harm them.

*f)* Nylon neither shrinks nor stretches however often it is washed, but it is affected by heat as it is a thermoplastic material, which means that it can be moulded with heat. Therefore it can be permanently embossed with patterns and it can be set into permanent pleats.

*g)* Nylon materials require very little ironing but most of them are the better for a slight touch up with the iron which should on no account be too hot or the fabric will melt — setting 2-warm $150^{\circ}$C.

*h)* Nylon yarn is of low flammability and will melt away from heat so that it is safe provided it does not have inflammable trimmings.

*i)* Colour can be introduced into the spinning solution. Colouring the yarn after spinning proved difficult at first and only those dyes suitable for acetate could be used, but further experiments proved that it can also be dyed easily with the same classes of dye used for wool.

*j)* Nylon is crease-resistant and is often mixed with other fibres to give them this quality plus extra strength and lightness and to enable the other fibres to be durably pleated.

*k)* It resists abrasion and when mixed with other fibres increases their resistance to abrasion.

*l)* When nylon materials are rubbed they acquire static electricity which is rather unfortunate because it causes the materials to pick up dirt and hold it. The hem of petticoats are particularly affected in this way as they collect the dust and dirt which rises from the ground and, unless washed daily, this soiling is difficult to remove completely and causes discoloration. However with the production of Celon which is anti-stat, this problem is now very greatly reduced.

*m)* Nylon is not attacked by bacteria, mildew or moth grubs.

*n)* It rots after long exposure to sunlight and so is not suitable for curtains.

*o)* The fineness of the fibre makes material woven from it very close and, as it is not absorbent, perspiration cannot evaporate and dries on the skin, necessitating an increased use of deodorants. Knitted fabric and those made from textured yarns are much better in this respect as the larger spaces between the stitches and the bulked yarn allow for evaporation.

**Identifying Nylon**

If the burning test is used nylon runs away from the flame and melts into a hard bead.

Under a microscope the yarn looks like a glass rod, quite smooth. When steeped in formic acid it dissolves.

*Cross-section*

Nylon Fibre
Microscopic diagram

### Celon (Nylon 6)

This is a new nylon made by Courtaulds Ltd. It is a slightly softer fibre than Bri-nylon (nylon 6.6). It has low flammability, a good elastic recovery and resists abrasion. It is mothproof and not damaged by bacteria. The fibre can be damaged by strong acids and by bleaches such as hydrogen of peroxide and chlorine bleach but is unaffected by alkalies and the usual dry-cleaning agents. It can be washed by hand or in a washing machine (white fabrics in hot water, 60°C and coloured fabrics in cooler, hand-hot water 48°C.) It may be spin-dried for 15 seconds and safely tumbler dried. The melting point of Celon is lower than that of nylon 6.6; therefore the ironing temperature should be cool (setting 2 on the new irons and silk or nylon setting on the older types).

To test if fabric is Celon, place a scrap on a slow hotplate with a scrap of nylon 6.6. Celon will melt first.

A fluorescent white is introduced into all white nylon and after a time, wear and washing causes nylon 6.6 to turn yellowish but Celon holds the white much better. Long exposure to sunlight can cause loss of strength but no yellowing.

Celon is, at present, used mostly for knitted fabrics for lingerie, nylon shirtings, dresses and stretch slacks and socks. Brushed Celon has a soft silky handle and bulked Celon is similar in appearance to Crimplene.

The yarn can also be woven into taffetas, crepes, georgettes and voiles and into rainwear fabrics.

### Enkalon

Enkalon is also a nylon 6 fibre, made by British Enkalon Ltd.

### POLYESTER FIBRE

Terylene is one of the fibres in this group. Fabrics made from it are particularly suited to the times in which we live. They may be featherweight, are easy to wash, and are quick-drying, crease-resistant and hardwearing, and suitable for most purposes.

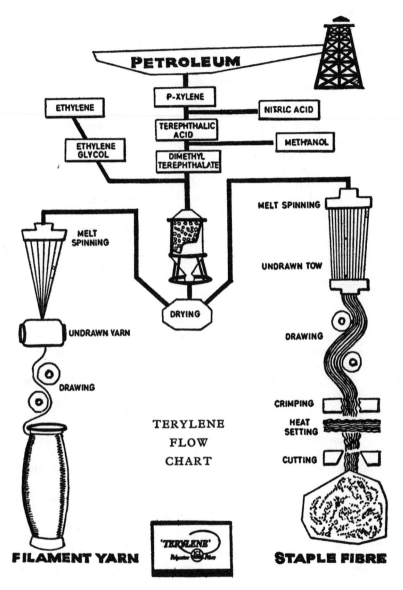

TERYLENE
FLOW
CHART

FILAMENT YARN

STAPLE FIBRE

An Example of Polyester Fibre Production
Reproduced by courtesy of Imperial
Chemical Industries Ltd.

*Production*

*a)* Polyester fibre is made from ethylene glycol and terephthalic acid, both of which are obtained from petroleum. They go through complicated chemical processes to form a polyester.

*b)* The polyester is run on to a roller on which it cools into an ivory-like solid polymer.

*c)* The polymer is cut up into small chips.

*d)* The chips are melted at a high temperature to make the spinning solution.

*e)* When forced through the spinneret, the filaments harden in the air and are made into yarn which is wound on to cylinders.

*f)* The yarn is drawn, that is, stretched, to several times its original length and wound on to bobbins. This is the silky filament yarn. It is sent to textile manufacturers who make it into fabrics such as those used for lingerie.

*g)* Staple fibre is produced in a similar way except that many more filaments are combined to make a 'tow'. This is drawn, crimped, set by heat and then cut into suitable staple lengths for blending with other fibres and is more important in this form.

## The Properties of Polyester Fibre

*a)* It is strong, tough, and wears well.

*b)* It is as strong when wet as it is when dry.

*c)* It resists acids and bleaches better than most other fibres and is not harmed by alkalies unless they are in strong solution at a high temperature. Washing is easy — use hand-hot water, a cold rinse and drip-dry.

*d)* It does not absorb water, and if hung up to dry needs little or no ironing but, if it is wrung out when hot and wet, creases may have to be ironed out afterwards.

*e)* It is thermoplastic and so can be permanently pleated.

*f)* It is flame-resistant.

*g)* It is crease-resistant and often used with other fibres to impart this quality.

*h)* It may be dry-cleaned safely.

*i)* It is not attacked by moth grubs, silver fish, white ants, fungi, mildew or bacteria.

*j)* Unlike nylon, it is not harmed by sunlight, particularly if it comes through glass, so it is particularly suitable for curtains.

*k)* It resists abrasion.

*l)* It is subject to static electrification. Dirt and dust may be attracted and garments should be washed frequently.

*m)* It is not easy to dye, unless special methods are used, and therefore cannot be dyed in the home.

*n)* It can be used for many purposes, e.g. hoses, tyres, belting cloth, awnings, industrial clothing, suitings, dainty dress materials, net, lace, sewing thread, down-like filling for eiderdowns and pillows, etc.

*o)* It is not quite so elastic as nylon.

**Identifying Polyester**

Polyester will dissolve in concentrated sulphuric acid. The burning test fuses the fabric into a hard bead. It is difficult to set alight but will eventually burn with a yellow flame and give off an aromatic smell. In Great Britain, polyester fibre is manufactured by Imperial Chemical Industries Ltd. and sold under the trade name 'Terylene', and by Courtaulds under the name of Lirelle.

Polyester fibre is made in other countries under different names.

Polyester Fibre
Microscopic diagram

## ACRYLIC FIBRES

These are called acrylic fibres as they are made, in the first instance, from acrylonitrile, obtained from coal carbonization and natural gas found in oil wells. This is made into a polymer which is dissolved in a solvent so that it can be spun into filaments. The filaments are combined into a tow which is given a crimp and then cut into staple lengths. Always in staple form it can either be spun into yarn, to be used by itself, or it can be blended with other fibres, The yarn can be knitted or woven into lovely, soft, luxurious fabrics. Originally Acrilan was produced in America but is now being made in Northern Ireland by Chemstrand Ltd. Courtelle is made by Courtaulds Ltd.

Other acrylic fibres are: Orlon made by Du Pont (UK) Ltd. and Acrilan made by Monsanto Textiles Ltd.

**Properties of Acrylic Fibres**

*a)* The crimping in the fibres causes the yarn to contain pockets of air which make materials warm to wear. It is claimed that they are as warm as wool.
*b)* The yarn is used to make a variety of fabrics — very fine materials, light in weight or heavier ones for warmer wear, fabrics with a pile, blankets which are soft and warm without being heavy, and even carpets. The materials are suitable for dresses, jersey dresses, sweaters, children's wear, sports shirts, suitings, industrial overalls, raincoats. Courtelle fleece makes warm linings and dressing-gowns.

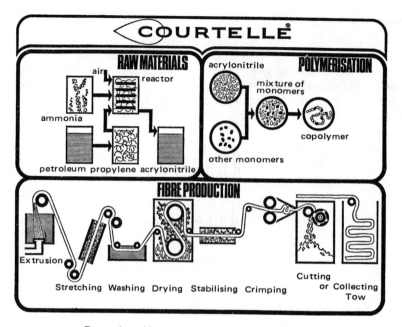

Reproduced by courtesy of Courtaulds Ltd.

*c)* Fabrics are strong with a crisp, or soft as cashmere, feel. They may be dull, lustrous, smooth — everything from fleece to soft jersey.

*d)* Both wash very well in warm water (on no account should they be boiled as the fibre will be harmed). They retain their shape, neither shrinking nor stretching. They are not very absorbent so will drip-dry quickly and require very little ironing. The iron should be cool and they should be ironed dry, because they will stretch if ironed damp.

*e)* They can be permanently pleated and give this quality to fabrics in which they are blended with other fibres, provided 50 per cent of either yarn is present.

*f)* They are unharmed by the usual dry-cleaning agents.

*g)* Resistant to acids and not harmed by alkalies at low temperatures.

*h)* Not harmed unduly by bleaches.

*i)* Neither is affected by sunlight.

*j)* Neither is affected by mildew nor attacked by moth grubs, making other fibres with which they are blended mothproof.

*k)* Materials drape beautifully and are easy to sew.

*l)* Materials are not irritating to the skin.

*m)* They are crease-shedding.

**Tests for Acrylic Fibres**

When the burning test is used the fabric melts into a tar-like black bead and shrivels away from the flame. Acrylics dissolve in concentrated nitric acid. Microscopic cross-sections of the fibres have various forms as shown in the following diagrams.

Cross-section Courtelle     Cross-section Orlon     Cross-section Acrilan
Microscopic diagram     Microscopic diagram     Microscopic diagram

## MODIFIED ACYLIC FIBRES

These are acrylic fibres which have been modified to make them flame-retardant and it is hoped that they will become increasingly more important. They have the same properties as acrylics but are more affected by heat. Teklan is a staple fibre made by Courtaulds which satisfies the British Standards for 'flame-proof' fabrics. It is very useful for children's nightwear, for furnishing fabrics and industrial overalls. If it is used round a core of glass fibre it becomes one of the safest flame-proof fabrics made.

The flame-resistance withstands repeated washing and dry-cleaning. Use a COOL iron.

*Dynel* is another acrylic fibre made in America.

Dynel
Microscopic diagram

## OLEFIN FIBRES

There are two types of olefin fibres — polyethylene and polypropylene. Both derive from the petroleum industry. They have special uses and are quite different from other fibres.

*Polyethylene*

This was the first of these fibres to be used as a textile, by Courtaulds, who produced a fibre called **Courlene.**

## Properties of Courlene

*a)* It is absolutely non-absorbent.

*b)* Very resistant to alkalies, acids and chemicals which makes fabric woven from it most suitable for overalls in chemical industries.

*c)* Can be cleaned by sponging or wiping down with soap-suds or by using carbon tetrachloride.

*d)* As it has a low melting point high temperatures will damage fabrics and they should never be ironed.

*e)* Often used to interline semi-stiff collars as it softens with heat and will fuse the material into permanent stiffness.

*f)* The colours remain fast and it does not rot.

## Uses

On account of its toughness and the ease with which it can be cleaned, it is used to make fabrics for upholstery and car seats. It is woven in gay patterns and used for deck-chair covers, for which it is particularly suitable, as it does not absorb rain in bad weather and can be wiped dry. For this reason it is also used for bathroom covers and for curtains for showers.

*Polypropylene*

Like polyethylene this fibre is quite non-absorbent and has a low melting point. It can be used to make the knitted backing of 'fur fabrics' in which the pile is held. It is also used as a slit fibre, that is a ribbon-like fibre which is stretched and twisted into string and rope.

Imperial Chemical Industries Ltd. make a staple polypropylene fibre called Spunstron and British Celanese Ltd., a monofilament called Cournova. There are many other firms also making the same types of fibre.

## Ulstron *(Polypropylene Fibre)*

This is made in the United Kingdom by Imperial Chemical Industries Ltd. from propylene gas derived from oil. It can be a plastic or a fibre in filament or staple form.

Properties of the fibre:

1) Very strong, both wet and dry.

2) Very light — the lightest fibre known.
3) Has outstanding resistance to chemicals, most acids and alkalies.
4) Rot proof.
5) Absorbs less moisture than polyester and nylon.
6) High resistance to abrasion.
7) Has a low melting point, therefore care must be taken when fabric made from it needs ironing.
8) Staple fibres are very soft and warm.

It is used for making blankets, which on account of its lightness are, weight for weight, warmer than other blankets constructed in the same way. It is also used for fur and pile fabrics, protective clothing, upholstery fabrics and for carpets.

## POLYVINYL CHLORIDE (*Plastic Sheeting*)

Strictly speaking this is not a textile but we do stitch it up to make such articles as toilet bags, hanging wardrobes, raincoats, aprons, curtains, and so on.

The plastic sheeting can be obtained in various thicknesses and it is non-porous and completely non-absorbent. It can be printed in attractive patterns and colours or it can be self-coloured throughout. The surface can be moulded into different textures, smooth, rough, grained, and so on. By themselves these sheetings are not particularly strong and will tear, especially where stitching perforates them. To make them stronger they can be backed with a light fabric to which they are fused. They have a low melting point and shrivel up and melt when heat is applied to them. They stiffen up in cold temperatures and become soft again when they are warmed. In time, some of them tend to become less flexible and discoloured.

## ELASTANE FIBRES (*Polyurethane*)

These are special elastic yarns which are taking the place of rubberised elastic. They are made from segmented polyurethane which is obtained from the petro-chemical industry. They were first made in America where they were called 'Spandex' yarns, but in Europe they are now referred to as elastomeric yarns. The various manufacturers have their own trade names for their own yarns, thus Du Pont make **Lycra** and Courtaulds Ltd. make **Spanzelle**.

### Properties of Elastane Fibres
1) They have a high degree of elasticity.
2) The elastic recovery is good — better than that of extruded rubber.
3) They are unharmed by perspiration, soap, detergents, deodorants, sun-tan oils and many chemicals. Perspiration and detergents rot rubber, so having this advantage over rubber, elastomerics last very much longer.

4) They are filament yarns and can be spun into much finer deniers than can extruded rubber so that sheer fabrics can be made from them e.g. tights, stockings and fine tricots, which are very lightweight and comfortable to wear.
5) They take dye very well so that when fully stretched there is no loss of colour.

The yarn can be covered, as is extruded rubber, and can be used to produce a warp stretch or a weft stretch or a two-way stretch in woven fabrics, and is also used for knitted fabrics. It can be used with other fibres to make fabrics where stretch and quick recovery is required. One disadvantage is that fabrics are rather expensive compared with rubberised elastic but this is somewhat offset by the fact that they last so very much longer. Fabrics made from these yarns are used for outer garments, socks, corsetry and swimwear. Spanzelle is particularly suitable for swimwear as it resists chlorinated water while Vyrene can be harmed by chlorine.

## METAL THREAD FABRICS

For evening wear many fabrics are made incorporating metal threads to make them glitter and sparkle. In heavy, high quality lamé materials a gold or silver coloured metal thread is used, and unfortunately this tarnishes and garments made from it have to be carefully stored in coloured tissue paper in dress boxes or, better still, in plastic bags which help to exclude the tarnishing agents in air. Metal thread fabrics need to be stitched carefully as the metal thread is coarser than the yarn from which the fabric is mainly made and therefore a very sharp, fine machine needle must be used. Blunt, thick needles would catch on the metal thread and pull it, possibly distorting the pattern on the fabric. If the metal thread is used to produce a spray of flowers here and there on a plain background it is carried across the background rather loosely on the underside, and unless the material is handled carefully it is very easy to pluck it so that the metal thread stands up in small loops where one does not want it to. The fabric tends to be rather 'scratchy' on the inside particularly on the cut edges of the seams so that for comfort in wear garments should be lined and the seam edges bound with crossway strips. However, nowadays Lurex thread is widely used and this is a soft, smooth, lightweight thread, gold, silver or coloured, which does not tarnish and is quite comfortable to wear. It is much easier to sew.

All metal thread fabrics should be dry-cleaned.

### Glitter Threads

These threads are flat and ribbon-like, made from tinted plastic which glitters. They are made in one of two ways: *(a)* by cutting a flat sheet into strips, or *(b)* by forcing the liquid through spinnerets with flat slits in them instead of holes.

## GLASS FIBRE

Molten glass can be pulled out into fine threads to make yarn for fabric. To begin with it was rather brittle and difficult to use but further experiments have improved it and it is now used to make attractive fabrics for curtains.

Glass yarn is made from silica and various oxides such as silicon dioxide, calcium oxide, aluminium oxide, boron oxide, magnesium oxide, sodium and potassium oxide.

*a)* These ingredients are mixed together and melted in a furness at about 2500°F. The glass is then drawn into fibres (Direct Melt Process) or made into marbles (Marble Process).

*b)* The marbles are re-melted in a tank and by gravity the liquid is fed through small holes in the bottom of the tank to form filaments.

*c)* The filaments are pulled out to the required thickness.

*d)* Because glass is brittle a binder made from starch and oil is applied and makes a lubricant coating round each filament as it leaves the tank.

*e)* The filaments are then twisted together into yarn. The thickness of the final yarn depends on the number of holes in the tank (i.e. the number of filaments), the liquidity of the melted glass and the speed with which the thread is drawn out.

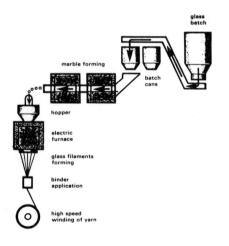

Glass Yarn Manufacture
Reproduced by courtesy of Courtaulds

**Properties**

1) It has a silky, slightly brittle feel.
2) It drapes well and curtains should be fairly full so that they may hang gracefully.
3) It neither shrinks nor stretches.
4) Colours are fairly fast.
5) It is not rotted by sunlight.
6) It is not attacked by mildew or moths.
7) It is not inflammable, quite an important point with curtains.
8) It is not absorbent and dries within a few minutes after washing and requires no ironing. It must be washed gently by hand and not in a washing machine.
9) It should not be allowed to rub against rough window sills or venetian blinds.

# 3 Yarn Types

In the preceding chapter mention was made of the two main types of yarn, namely continuous filament and staple yarns. Both types of yarn are usually twisted — so many twists per centimetre, according to the type of yarn required.

Yarn made from short staple fibres needs more twists than that made from longer fibres as the purpose of the twist is to hold together the overlapping ends of the short fibres down the length of the yarn so that when strain is put on the yarn the fibres grip and cling to each other and do not pull apart. In filament yarn the twist is not needed to hold the long strands together but can be introduced to make crêpe yarns. The amount of twist is important in producing different types of yarn. A loosely twisted yarn is soft and has lustre and warmth. A tightly twisted yarn is dull and springy and the more twists it has the more elastic it becomes. The 'happy medium' between the two gives normal yarn.

When twisted clockwise the yarn has an S twist, see diagram. Twisted anti-clockwise it has a Z twist.

A SINGLE YARN consists of one or more filament yarns twisted into a single thread (monofilament) or it can be a single thread of staple yarn.

A FOLDED or PLY YARN is made up of two or three single yarns twisted together (two-fold or three-fold).

A CABLE YARN has two folded yarns twisted together and is used to make heavier industrial types of fabric.

If an S twist yarn is folded with a Z twist one the folded yarn becomes strong and lustrous.

The direction of these twists in the yarn is used to produce different effects in fabrics, for example, crêpe yarn can be woven from tightly twisted yarn by using alternate pairs of S and Z twisted weft threads.

S Twist          Z Twist

## MIXTURES AND BLENDS

There is a distinct difference between a fabric which is made from a mixture of yarns and one that is made from yarn which has been blended.

*Mixtures.* The fabric is woven from different types of yarn which are separate and distinct; for example, the warp threads may be polyester yarn and the weft threads, which are woven in and out of them, may be of cotton yarn.

*Blends.* In this instance a composite yarn is made from two or more different fibres and the fabric is woven or knitted from this one yarn. Yarns may be blended in different ways as follows:

*a)* Several varieties of staple fibres, for example, 14% wool 72% cotton and 14% protein fibres may be mixed and spun together to make the yarn.

*b)* A wool yarn may be folded with a cotton yarn.

*c)* Filament blend yarns are made by mixing together the spinning solutions of man-made fibres before extruding them through the spinneret so that they emerge as one composite yarn; for example, Tricel and Celon solutions mixed produce Tricelon yarn.

*Core Spun Yarn.* This kind of blended yarn has a central core of one fibre which is encased in another fibre. In this way strength can be given to a weaker yarn; for example, an outer covering of woollen fibres can enclose a nylon filament core and this will strengthen the wool without altering its appearance. Elastane yarns are also core spun.

*Wrapped yarns.* Elastic has a rubber core which is completely disguised by being wrapped around with yarn.

## FANCY YARNS

In order to produce interesting textures and effects in fabrics yarns can be adapted to make the following types.

*a)* A *slub yarn* is one which is alternately thick and thin. Extra staple fibre is spun into it at intervals to cause the thickening. Viscose filament yarn can also be slubbed by forcing the spinning solution through the spinneret in increased quantities every now and again to make the filaments thicker at intervals. Fabric woven from slub yarn has raised streaks of thicker thread irregularly placed here and there throughout.

*b)* A *knop yarn* is similar to a slub but in place of thickened streaks it has small knops spun into it at regular intervals and fabric made from it has small bumps on the surface.

*c)* *Bouclé yarn* is twisted into loops facing upwards and downwards alternately as in the diagram.

*d)* *Grandelle yarn* is made from yarns of different colours folded together, and shaded colour effects can be obtained by varying the amount of twist used in the folding process. This yarn is used mainly for worsteds and suiting.

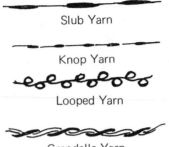

Slub Yarn

Knop Yarn

Looped Yarn

Grandelle Yarn

## TEXTURED, BULKED AND STRETCH YARNS

Man-made filament yarns take the temperature of the atmosphere, being stuffy on hot days and chilly on cold days; so they are textured and bulked by fluffing up to give warmth, absorbency and comfort in wear. Stretch and elasticity can be given to synthetic yarns by special processes. Some yarns, e.g. nylon, polyester and acetate, are thermoplastic, that is, they can be softened by heat and moulded into different shapes. If they are crimped or twisted and then subjected to heat they will thereafter retain the twist or crimp so that if they are pulled out straight and then released they will spring back again into the twisted or crimped form. The amount of stretch can be controlled depending on how tightly they are twisted or how much they are crimped. It should be pointed out here that, if a greater heat than was used to produce the twist or crimp is applied to fabrics made from these yarns, as for instance, during ironing, the yarn may be permanently straightened out and so lose its stretch. Therefore particular attention should be paid to washing and ironing instructions.

*Agilon nylon yarn.* A bulked yarn with a good deal of stretch. Filament yarn is heated and is pulled over a sharp edge, and this gives it a coil-like springiness. The yarn will pull out straight and spring back again every time. This spiral spring gives materials made from the yarn a softness and a definite warmth because insulating air is caught between the coils. Also it dulls the lustre giving a very pleasing effect to fabrics. It can be used for stockings, tights and knitted and woven materials.

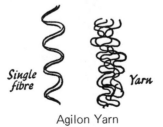

*Single fibre*          *Yarn*

Agilon Yarn

*Ban-lon nylon yarns (Tycora).* Bulked yarns which will stretch. The yarn is packed tightly in a heated stuffer box to set it into a zig-zag form and when several threads are combined the zig-zagging holds them away from each other and considerable amounts of air are trapped between them. This yarn makes a fabric with a matt surface which is warm and soft and very light in weight.

It washes well and keeps its shape, neither stretching nor shrinking, and it dries quickly. It is suitable for such underwear as vests and pants and for socks, jumpers, cardigans, jersey dresses and many other types of dress material, lace and brocade.

Ban-lon Yarn

*Crimped or crêpe yarn.* Thermoplastic yarn is twisted tightly in one direction and set by heat, then untwisted and doubled with a yarn in which the filaments are twisted in the opposite direction. This makes a very elastic yarn suitable for the stretch type of stockings and socks and for swimsuits and lingerie. 'Fluflon' and 'Helanca' are trade names for nylon yarns crimped in special ways.

Crêpe Yarn

*False-twist crimping.* Yarn is twisted, set by heat and untwisted, in the opposite direction, by a false-twist spindle, making it loop; and, to prevent it tangling up, it is doubled with yarn twisted the other way. Crimplene is made like this.

*'Moygashel' Expando Fabric.* This is a stretch fabric made from 92½% spun rayon and 7½% nylon. The stretch runs across the weft from selvedge to selvedge. The warp is spun rayon which does not stretch and the nylon is crimped and is pulled out straight during the weaving and relaxes back into crimps during dyeing and finishing, thus producing the stretch. This is a linen-like fabric suitable for tight jeans and slacks. It 'gives' with the body movements and does not 'bag' at the knees. 'Moygashel' Fleriflax is a similar weft stretch fabric made from a mixture of crimped nylon and flax.

Stretch denim is also made and this also is suitable for slacks.

*Taslan yarn.* Yet another way to bulk yarn but in this case no elasticity is added. It is most suitable for woven materials but knitted fabric can be made from it. The yarn is passed through a strong current of air which causes each of the filaments making up the yarn to form small loops at irregular intervals. As the loops in each strand come in different places they are held in position by the other filaments. The loops trap air and fabric made from this yarn is very soft, warm and light in weight. Any thickness of yarn can be treated in this way to make fabrics of different weights suitable for shirts, blouses, dresses and furnishings. Different textures can be produced by varying the size of the loops, by mixing other fibres with the yarn or by mixing taslan-treated yarn with a smooth one and so on. Any filament yarn can be taslan-textured.

Taslan Yarn

*Crinkle yarns*
a) Knit-de-knit method. Yarn is knitted, set with heat and then unravelled, producing a crinkle or bouclé appearance.
b) Gear crimping. A quicker method in which the yarn is passed between two heated interlocking cog wheels to make it wavy. No stretch is added by either method.

*High Bulk Process.* Method a) Acrylic fibres which shrink different amounts are spun together. During finishing those which shrink most will cause the others to bulk up. In method b) two acrylic fibres which shrink differently are blended to form a composite yarn and the fibre which shrinks most will bulk up the other one. Such yarns are 'Latent Crimp Courtelle', 'Bi-component Acrilan' and 'Orlon Sayelle'.

I.C.I. are making a polyester yarn with a higher shrinkage rate to blend with standard polyester and the resultant yarn is known as 'Terylene-plus T' and 'Terylene 75'.

## COUNTS & DENIER NUMBERS AND THE TEX SYSTEM

Formerly a 'count' or a denier number was used to show how fine or coarse a yarn was. A 'count' was used for cotton, worsted, wool and linen yarns and a denier number for filament yarns. Most people will know that à 15 denier stocking is finer than a 30 denier one.

Nowadays the TEX SYSTEM is being used, to conform with European standards.

A tex number equals the weight in grammes of 1000 metres of cotton, worsted, wool or linen yarn in place of the 'count'. A decitex number equals the weight in grammes of 10,000 metres of filament yarn in place of the denier number.

The higher the tex or decitex number the coarser the yarn.

# 4 From Yarn to Fabric

In this day and age we are very fortunate to have so many different yarns with which to make lovely materials for our clothes and furnishings, when we consider with how little our early ancestors had to make do. Today we make some materials by much the same methods as they used only we have invented machines to help us to do what they did by hand or with very crude tools. We use three main methods for making fabrics: weaving, knitting and felting. Each method makes quite a different type of material suitable for different purposes.

## WOVEN MATERIALS

Weaving is one of the oldest ways of making cloth and is suitable for all kinds of yarn. It is carried out on a loom which, nowadays, is a complicated piece of machinery. In the beginning, fabric was woven in its simplest form as follows:

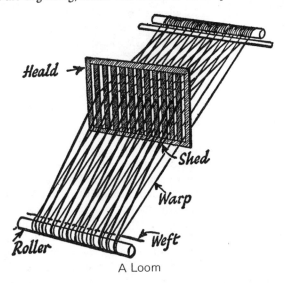

A Loom

1) Lengthwise threads, called *warp threads*, were arranged and wound on rollers — one at each end of the loom. These threads have to be strong to withstand the strain of weaving.

2) The warp threads were threaded through a *heald*, which was made of wooden strips in a frame. Each strip had a hole in the centre and a space between it and its neighbour. The warp was threaded alternately through the holes and the spaces. See diagram.

59

3) When the heald was raised, the threads through the holes were lifted above those threaded through the spaces, forming a passage between them. This passage was called a *shed*.

4) Yarn was wound on a shuttle and this was passed through the shed. This yarn was called the *weft*.

5) The heald was then pushed down until the warp threads through the holes were below those threaded through the spaces, forming a new shed, and the shuttle containing the weft was passed back through it.

The rigid heald was pressed up against each weft row as it was made to push the threads close to each other. As the weaving proceeded the cloth was wound on to the front roller until all the warp, which was originally wound on the back roller was used up.

This made a *plain* or *tabby* weave in which the weft threads passed over and under one warp thread alternately.

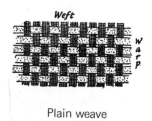

Plain weave

As weaving progressed the heald was changed and was made with strings, with loops in the centre, threaded on the wooden frame and later, wire was used in place of the string. Then more than one heald was used. The advantage of this was, that if the warp was threaded through them in a set order, groups of warp threads could be lifted or depressed at one time to form the shed so that the weft could pass over or under several warp threads in each row, and, in this way, a woven pattern could be produced. The warp could be threaded through the healds in many different orders and with the use of coloured yarns, countless patterns, in both weave and colour could be made. This method is still in use today. When the healds are made with string or metal they are not rigid nor strong enough to press the weft rows against each other and a special beater called a *reed* is used for this purpose. It looks like a fine metal grill and the warp is threaded through each space in it after it has passed through the healds. The reeds are used also to control the fineness of the cloth because they are made in different sizes, for example, one will make a fabric with six warp threads to the cm, whereas another will make a finer cloth, ten or more threads to the cm.

The weft threads need not be so strong as the warp, though sometimes they are of the same thickness when an even-weave material is required, and they can be thicker, depending on the desired effect.

## Jacquard Loom

Later a much more complicated loom was invented called a Jacquard loom. In this each warp thread can be lifted by itself, independently of all the others and most elaborate patterns can be made. Damasks and brocades are all made on this type of loom and the colour and pattern are produced entirely by the weaving.

The following are some of the more usual weaves:

## Basket or Hopsack Weave

Two rows of weft threads pass alternately over and under two warp threads. The material known as hopsack is woven in this way.

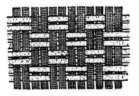

Basket or Hopsack weave

## Haircord Weave

This weave produces a slight ribbed effect.
*1st row:* The weft passes over two and under one warp thread alternately.
*2nd row:* The weft passes under two and over one warp. These two rows are repeated throughout.

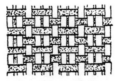

Haircord weave

**Twill Weave**

This gives a noticeable diagonal rib across the material. Cotton drill is one example. The weft passes over and under two warp threads alternately but, in each row, the weft thread is moved one warp thread forward.

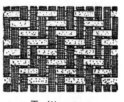

Twill weave

**Dogstooth Weave**

A distinctive weave, often used for tweeds. It is usually a twill weave, using two colours, four rows of each alternately, in both the warp and the weft.

Dogstooth weave

**Herringbone Weave**

Another weave often used for tweeds, producing a zigzag effect.

*1st row:* The weft passes over one warp and under five.

*2nd row:* The weft passes under one warp, over one, under three and over one.

*3rd row:* The weft passes under two warps and afterwards continues, over one, under one, over one, under three.

*4th row:* Begins under three and then continues, over one and under five alternately.

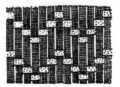

Herringbone

## Satin Weave

The shiny effect of satin is obtained by having long warp threads as unbroken as possible by weft threads.

*1st row:* The weft is taken over one warp and under four alternately.

*2nd row:* Begins under three and then continues over one and under four alternately.

*3rd row:* Begins under one and continues over one and under four alternately.

*4th row:* Under four and over one.

*5th row:* Begins under two and continues over one and under four alternately.

Satin weave

## Crêpe Fabrics

These fabrics have a characteristic pebble surface. The best quality crêpe fabrics are woven from highly twisted yarn in a plain weave with two weft threads with a S twist alternating with two having a Z twist. The more twisted the yarn, the more it will shrink and as the cloth is slightly stretched in finishing, care must be taken when making up woollen crêpe fabrics. If too much moisture is used during pressing the garment may shrink to a smaller size than it was when it was cut out.

Untwisted yarn can be used to make crêpe fabrics and for these a special crêpe weave is used. These fabrics are less likely to shrink.

Moss crêpe differs from other crêpe fabrics in that it is made from twisted viscose yarn folded with an untwisted acetate yarn and then woven in a moss crêpe weave. The texture is quite different and the fabric has a tendency to fray when handled.

### PILE FABRICS

Pile fabrics have a raised surface which may be cut warp or weft threads, looped warp threads, brushed or tufted. Examples are velvets, corduroy, terry towelling, face cloths and fur fabrics. For convenience brushed fabrics are included in this section, though strictly speaking they do not have a pile but rather a 'nap'.

Velvets are made from silk or nylon, velveteens and corduroys from cotton or viscose yarns.

**Velvet**

The following are two methods of producing the pile. (1) Two layers of material are woven, face to face, with a space between them and are connected to each other with warp threads running across the space. When the weft threads have been woven in, the warp threads connecting the two fabrics are cut through and form the pile, so that two lengths of material are woven at the same time.
(2) This time a single length of material is woven and warp threads looped over wires which have a knife edge attached to them. After weaving, the knife cuts through the loops leaving them in closely packed tufts. If an uncut pile is required the wires are withdrawn without cutting the threads and the pile is left in loops.

After weaving the pile is sheared level to give it the characteristic bloom and then it is treated by brushing and steaming to make the type of fabric required. For example, the pile can be upright, or it can be pressed in one direction as in panne velvet, or in several directions as in crushed velvet.

*Façonné or brocaded velvet* has a sheer, plain background with only the pattern in a raised velvet pile. This effect is obtained by printing the background with chemicals to dissolve away the unwanted pile without affecting the ground fabric which is made from fibres resistant to the chemicals.

*Velveteen* is made from cotton on a cotton backing and here the pile is made from the weft threads. An extra weft thread lies on top of the surface of the fabric and is caught into the base at intervals so that it floats loose across several warp threads between each anchoring. After weaving the floats are cut.

*Corduroy or corded velvet*, also made from cotton, is made in the same way as velveteen with the floating weft threads arranged so that they run in even rows down the length of the fabric. When cut they form the ribbed pile.

Some velvets are made from knitted satin fabric brushed to produce a nap.

*Terry towelling* is made differently from velvet. It has a special weave where extra pile-warp threads which are slack, are anchored into the base fabric, forming loops on both sides. These loops remain uncut.

*Brushed nap surfaces* are produced by brushing the surface of the fabric with teazles or wire brushes. This raises the surface into a smooth nap.

*Fur fabric* usually has a cotton knitted base into which looped yarns of other fibres are inserted in much the same way as wool is looped into hessian to make rugs. The loops are then cut and brushed out so that they conceal the base cloth.

## KNITTED MATERIALS

Knitted fabric is becoming increasingly popular because it is comfortable to wear and crease-shedding. Most types of yarn can be used and the man-made fibres with their stretch properties give increased elasticity and comfort in wear. Examples of knitted fabrics are cotton locknit, wool jersey, nylon tricot, courtelle jersey and so on.

## a) Weft Knitting

This is like hand knitting, working across the width of the fabric and back. Each row of stitches is linked into the row above and below. Often these fabrics are knitted on circular machines producing a tube of fabric which sometimes helps to make cutting out more economical as it can be folded around in different places. Sometimes tubular fabric is slit and opened out into a single layer. The fabric needs careful stitching to keep its elastic quality and to prevent laddering. Many fabrics can be made from weft knitting, of which the following are a few.

*Double jersey fabrics.* These are ribbed, one plain, one purl, or two and two ribs. Both sides look alike and the fabric is suitable for cuffs and welts and whole garments.

*Double jersey interlock.* Two double jersey fabrics are connected together by two yarns knitted into them. The fabric is reversible.

*Plated fabric.* Made by knitting together two yarns so that the loops of one of the yarns lie exactly behind those of the other. When a patterned fabric is required the yarns can be of different colours and interchanged during the knitting.

*Brushed fabrics* have a straight, thick yarn threaded weftwise through the knitting stitches on the underside and the right side is brushed up to make a nap.

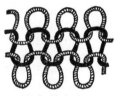

Weft Knitting

## b) Warp Knitting

This is made differently. Threads are arranged like warp threads in weaving and are looped into each other sideways across the fabric, forming upright ribs on the right side and horizontal ribs on the underside.

*Nylon tricot* is such a fabric. It is used for nightwear, lingerie and as a laminated lining for many fabrics.

*Cotton locknit.* This is made so that the stitches lock at the back and do not ladder and is used for underwear and sports shirts. This type of fabric can be made from yarns other than cotton.

*Raschel fabrics* are a special type of warp knitting. They vary from lacy fabrics to pile and heavier ones and from crochet-type trimmings to net curtaining.

*Weft inserts.* Yarn made from spun staple fibres such as slub or bouclé yarn is worked into warp knitted fabrics across the weft. It can produce interesting surface effects, sometimes making the fabric look as though it was woven, or giving it the appearance of tweed.

## LACE

Lace is made quite differently from woven fabrics and in early times could only be made by hand. There were two ways of making it:

a) *Embroidery.* Threads were looped together and strengthened with buttonhole stitch and other threads were darned in to make the patterns.

b) *Bobbin lace.* This lace was worked on a pillow stuck with pins outlining the pattern. The thread, wound on wooden or bone bobbins, was twisted round the pins in various sequences to make the pattern. This method is still worked by hand today as a craft.

These two methods could be combined — a net background being made by the bobbin method with the design embroidered in by means of needle and thread.

In 1808 John Heathcoat patented a machine to make net in which bobbins swung from right to left, twisting the threads together into a diamond mesh net on which designs were embroidered, still by hand. Today the Heathcoat firm make plain and decorative nets from cotton yarns and man-made fibres, including elastane fibres. They also make Tulle, which is net made from silk.

### Bobbin Net

Bobbin net can be made more interesting in several ways. Point d'Esprit is a name given to net with little spots worked all over it at intervals.

Flock-printed net is made by printing the pattern in lacquer on to the net. Powdered flock is then blown over it and adheres to the lacquer, leaving a raised velvet-like design when the surplus flock has been blown off. Gold and silver particles can be used in place of flock to give a metallic jewelled effect.

### Leavers Lace

Following on John Heathcoat's machine, John Leavers made another which not only made the background net but at the same time embroidered the design on to it. thus cutting out hand work. This lace is widely used today. It is made from three threads: warp, beam and bobbin threads. The warp threads are suspended and the bobbin thread swings like a pendulum between them, back and forth, while the beam thread moves across from right to left. The way the threads move is controlled by the pattern which is punched on a Jacquard card and in this way the threads are twisted and woven together to produce the desired design.

The yarn used for lace has to be of top quality and is especially processed. After the lace is made it goes through a starching process and is then pulled out to the correct finished width on a stentering machine and dried off in hot air.

Lace edgings are made in the same way as all-over lace, not in narrow strips but in rows of strips in a wide fabric which are separated afterwards.

Apart from all-over lace, Leavers lace can be obtained in the following forms:
*a) Flouncing,* which may be from 30.5 cm to 183 cm wide with one straight edge and one scalloped edge.
*b) Edgings,* which are narrow and have one straight edge and one ornamental one.
*c) Insertions,* which have both edges straight.
Ribbonhole insertions have slots at intervals through which ribbon can be threaded.
*d) Galloons,* which have both edges scalloped.
*e) Cut-out designs.* This is edging lace with deeply cut out ornamental borders.
*f) Re-embroidered lace,* which can be all-over or a trimming, and has the design motifs outlined with a heavy corded edge or with lurex worked by hand on an electric machine.

## Schiffli Embroidered Net Lace

This is made with a type of sewing machine which embroiders the pattern on to the net base. The machine has many stationary needles and the net is moved around over them by a Pantograph which follows the design which has been outlined on paper.
*Guipure lace* is really pure embroidery with a heavy, solid, padded appearance. It is worked by a Schiffli machine on to a background of acetate fabric which is soluble in acetone and which is dissolved away after the embroidery is completed. The design can be embroidered with any yarn which is unaffected by acetone.
Schiffli embroidery can be worked on any fabric to produce all-over embroidered fabric and trimmings for dresses, blouses and lingerie. An example is Broderie Anglaise.

## Barmen Lace

A different type of lace edging, sometimes called braid lace, is made in narrow widths from yarn on bobbins which interlace and plait the yarns together as they move about in pattern grooves in a circular plate.

# NON-WOVEN BONDED-FIBRE FABRICS

## Felt

This is made from wool fibres arranged in any order, not parallel but crossing each other in all directions for extra strength. The fibres are then wetted with soapy water and beaten up which causes the overlapping scales of wool fibres to interlock with each other to form a dense fabric. This is used for carpets, embroidery and hats.

### Bonded-Fibre Fabrics

Man-made fibres open up a wide field for bonded fabrics which are used for interlinings (e.g. Vilene) and for disposable sheets and dress fabrics.

A sheet or web of fibres or yarn is formed as wide as required and then by one means or another it is compacted or stitched into a fabric. Cotton and most of the man-made fibres may be used to make the web in one of the following ways:
a) Fibres are taken straight from the carding machine and are laid side by side. This makes a weak web as the fibres are all parallel down the length of the web.
b) Fibres are arranged in a criss-cross manner.
c) Some of the fibres are parallel and others cross them at an angle. This makes a stronger web.
d) Fibres are blown in a jet of air on to a perforated drum from which the web can be removed. In this instance the fibres become arranged evenly and completely at random.

After the web has been formed it is bonded into fabric in the following ways:
*a) Fusing.* Thermoplastic fibres are heated and pressed which causes them to melt and fuse together into a compact fabric. Fibres which are not thermoplastic can also be so bonded if they have a small percentage of thermoplastic fibres mixed with them.
*b) Adhesive method.* The web is immersed in, or sprayed or rolled with, synthetic rubber which will stick the fibres together.
*c) Needle bonding.* The web is punched through with barbed needles from both the top and the underside. The needles are at an angle and the barb catches some of the fibres in the web and carries them through so that the web is actually stitched together with its own fibres. Finally the fabric is brushed up to hide the needle punching. It is used for blankets.
*d) Stitch bonding.* (Arachne method) A web of fibres is fed into a warp knitting machine and the needles in the machine pick up viscose or nylon yarn from the underside, drawing it through the web to form rows of chain stitching down the length of the web (Malimo method). Loose warp and weft yarns (instead of fibres) are laid across each other and stitched with yarn which is knitted through them like warp knitting, to make dress, suit and curtain fabrics.

Sometimes a layer of scrim is sandwiched between two webs which are then stitch-bonded together.
*e) Spun Bonding.* Continuous filament yarns are arranged at random and where they cross are either stuck together with adhesive or, if the yarn is thermoplastic, fused with heat to form a sheet of fabric. Used for interlinings, wall coverings, backing for leather and laminating.

## LAMINATED FABRICS

Laminated fabrics consist of two or three layers of fabric stuck together. This may be done for the following reasons:

a) To make a lining unnecessary. For example, brushed nylon is laminated to a tricot backing for use as curtain fabric.

b) To provide an interlining.

c) To strengthen a weak fabric. For example, openwork lace can be laminated to net which adds strength without altering the appearance of the lace.

d) To give added warmth without weight. For example fabrics backed with foam and 'quilted' anorak materials.

e) To give warmth and provide a lining when foam is sandwiched between two fabrics.

f) To give interest to top coats by means of a reversible cloth when two fabrics, usually one plain and the other checked, are joined together.

g) To provide an easy way of applying decorative motifs.

The laminating is carried out as follows:

a) By using an acrylic polymer adhesive or a solution of polyurethene or polyester as adhesive. When the adhesive has been applied to both fabrics on the wrong side, they are stuck back to back and baked at $120^{\circ}$C to cement the bond.

When a heavy cloth is required the adhesive is applied all over the cloth but lighter fabrics which are required to drape well have the adhesive applied in spots or stripes by means of an engraved roller.

b) When foam is used either as a backing or as a sandwiched layer, it is passed quickly through gas flames to make the surfaces sticky so that they will adhere to the cloth.

c) Anorak material may have a sandwiched layer of wadding or foam which is laminated in a quilting pattern by heat and pressure.

d) Adhesive interlinings are also a form of lamination. Both woven and bonded-fibre interlinings are made with an adhesive substance applied to one side. Place the adhesive side to the wrong side of the fabric and press with a hot iron under a damp cloth. The adhesive becomes tacky with the heat and moisture and adheres to the cloth.

e) A fusible fleece is obtainable which is a web with a paper backing and provides a do-it-yourself means of laminating. For example decorative embroidered motifs can be applied to children's garments, tears can be invisibly mended in lace by laminating a net backing and hems can be fixed in place without stitching. The fleece is cut to the required size and shape and is placed face down on the wrong side of the motif and is then ironed on. The paper is peeled off leaving the web adhering to the motif which is placed right side up in position on the garment and pressed under a damp cloth with a hot iron.

## COATED FABRICS

Woven and knitted fabrics can be coated with P.V.C. which waterproofs them, making them suitable for watersport and rain wear, bags, hold-alls, and upholstery.

The patterned shiny fabric, often used for rain-coats, is made by a transfer method as follows:

a) Very smooth paper is coated with clear P.V.C.

b) The design is printed on to it.

c) This is then covered with another coating of P.V.C. and the cloth is applied to it. When the paper is removed the cloth has a glossy painted surface.

Simulated leather effects are obtained by coating knitted fabric, which is more flexible, with coloured P.V.C. and embossing the leather graining on it by means of engraved rollers.

# 5 Finishing Fabrics

After material has been made, some of it is a dirty 'grey' colour and it is unattractive and stiff so that it will not drape properly. Quite a lot has to be done to it before it is ready for the shops. The processes through which it goes from now on are known as finishing.

## 1) PURIFICATION

This means the cleaning and bleaching of materials to make them a pure white. The dirty grey colour is caused by the natural impurities in the fibres and also by the fact that they are usually treated with size, containing starch and oil, to help them to stand up to the strains and stresses of weaving. These substances have to be removed before the material can 'take' dye satisfactorily.

*Cotton* contains a natural greasy substance.

*Flax* contains fibrous matter which is tow-coloured and sometimes the yarn is bleached before it is woven.

*Silk* has the natural gum made by the silkworm to bind it together into the cocoon.

*Wool* is the dirtiest of all, containing natural oil and many impurities.

*Viscose* is the cleanest of all as, being man-made, it has no natural impurities but it has to be cleaned very carefully because of its weakness when wet.

## 2) SCOURING

This is the name given to the first purifying process which loosens the grease and impurities so that they can be washed out easily. The treatment has to vary according to the fibres because some of them are harmed by chemicals.

Cotton and linen are not weakened by alkalies or heat but care must be taken when using acids. Consequently they may be boiled safely with soda, caustic soda (both alkalies) and detergent, to dissolve the grease which is then washed out. The material must now be bleached pure white so that it may be dyed or printed any colour, and this is where care has to be taken because strong bleaches are acid and too much of them will weaken the fibres. Mild bleaching agents such as hydrogen peroxide or chlorine are used.

Silk and wool, unlike cotton, are weakened by alkalies so that only a weak one, such as ammonia, can be used to get rid of the gum and grease. They are bleached with either hydrogen peroxide or sulphur fumes.

Viscose has to have the size removed and is then washed before it can be dyed or printed.

Acetate is washed and if it is mixed with cotton fibres, which tend to go yellow in time, it is bleached with hydrogen peroxide.

Wet heat used to make man-made and synthetic fibres makes them yellowish. To obtain a pure white, as strong acid bleaches would weaken them, harmless fluorescent bleaches, which work with ultra-violet light to give a 'blueing' effect, are used.

## COLOURING FABRIC

When material has been purified it is ready to be coloured. Sometimes it is purified in yarn form and is dyed before being made into material. This has to be done when patterns are to be woven or knitted into material by means of different-coloured warp and weft threads, or stitches, as in the Fair Isle kind of knitting which is known as plaited knitting when used for making fabric.

### Plain Dyeing for Plain Coloured Fabric and Backgrounds

*a) Winch dyeing.* Fabric is looped over two rollers which revolve passing it back and forth through a dye bath between them or it is looped over one roller and dye is pumped through it.

*b) Pad dyeing.* Fabric passes through a dye bath, is then pressed between rollers and then the colour is set with heat or steam.

## PRINTING FABRIC

### Block Printing

A very slow and expensive method used only for exclusive materials, as it is carried out by hand. The design is traced on to wooden blocks, one for each colour, and the background is cut away, only that part being left in relief which is to be printed in the particular colour. This is the same principle as making a lino-cut or rubber stamp. The blocks are then inked and pressed in place on the material, great care being taken that the joins in the repeat of the pattern do not show.

### Roller Printing

This is a development of block printing, carried out by machinery. The pattern is engraved on to copper rollers, one for each colour, the difference being that the pattern is sunk instead of being raised. The material is fed between a revolving drum and the copper rollers, which touch the material and print the pattern on to it. Each roller is coloured by another roller just underneath it which picks up the colour from a tank below. On one side of each printing roller is a steel blade to scrape off the surplus coloured paste which would otherwise smudge the pattern and on the other side is another blade to scrape off the loose fluff and lint which would make the pattern print imperfectly. The copper rollers are expensive and the engraving is costly so this method is used only when there are enough orders for the particular pattern to make the expense worthwhile.

Roller printing can be carried out in three different ways:

*a) By direct printing* as described above.

*b) By resist printing.* Where a white pattern is required on a coloured background the patterned part is printed with a special substance which will not 'take' dye, but resists it, hence the name. Afterwards the material is dyed and the patterned parts remain white.

*c) By discharge printing.* Another way of printing a lighter pattern on a dark ground. First of all the ground colour is dyed into the material and then the pattern is printed on with the light colour mixed with a chemical. The chemical removes or discharges the background colour and leaves the light colour in its place.

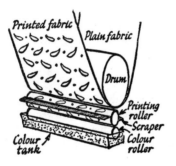

Rollor Printing

## Transfer Printing

This is a method which is becoming popular as it is more economical than roller printing. It is carried out by means of a transfer whereby all the colours can be printed at once, saving a succession of rollers. The pattern is printed on to paper in a medium which can be transferred to fabric with heat. By this method separate panels of fabric can be economically printed. It is widely used for printing knitted fabrics as these are of a stretchy nature and if separate rollers were used to print each colour, the smallest stretching of the fabric would result in the colours coming in not quite the right places. When all the colours can be transferred at a single printing this difficulty is overcome.

## Screen Printing

An attractive method in which any number of colours can be used. It is becoming very popular because, although it is carried out by hand, the cost of the screens is less than that of rollers and therefore more colours can be used more cheaply. The screens are made from silk or wire gauze stretched on wooden frames, one for each colour. The parts which are not to be printed are painted over with lacquer which stops the dye going through them, so that only the patterned part for each colour will print. The colour is pressed through with a rubber squeegee. Then the screen is lifted and placed in the next position. Each screen is worked by a different assistant and they follow on, one after the other, until all the colours have been printed.

After material has been coloured, by whichever method, it has to be steamed to fix the colours permanently.

## Flock Printing

This is quite a different way of getting a pattern on to fabric. By means of rollers the pattern is printed on with a gummy substance instead of with dye. Then a powdery flock is sprinkled over it and sticks to the gum and produces a raised pattern which resembles embroidery somewhat. This is quite durable and will stand up to washing without coming off.

## Stentering

During scouring, bleaching and dyeing or printing, the material is so pulled about that it becomes elongated and narrower than is required. To remedy this it is put through a stentering machine which has clips either side to grip the selvedges and pull the fabric out to the correct width.

## SPECIAL FINISHES

### Giving Lustre to Linen and Cotton

At this stage most fabrics have dull surfaces and cotton and linen are usually more popular if they are given a lustre.

*a) Calendering.* A finish used for cotton only. The material is polished in a machine called a friction calender, which resembles an outsize mangle with one wooden or metal roller and one made of softer material, such as paper or cotton, because if both were hard the material would be worn away with the friction. One roller moves round more quickly than the other and by friction polishes the material as it passes between them.

*b) Schreinering.* Another method which gives a very high sheen. The material passes between rollers which have been engraved with very fine lines and which are heated inside. The lines are imprinted on the fabric by the heat and catch the light and reflect it, giving the fabric a sheen.

*c) Roller embossing.* Patterns can be indented on rollers and these will imprint an embossed pattern on the fabric, which will reflect light on the raised parts. Unfortunately these methods are not washproof and after laundering the sheen and embossing will disappear unless the fabric is thermoplastic, when the finish can be set in permanently with heat.

*d) Beetling.* A method used for linen. The beetling machine has a lot of wooden hammers which beat the material giving it its characteristic lustre.

*e) Mercerized cotton.* This is a special finish which can be carried out when the cotton is in yarn form or after it has been made up into material. It will be remembered that the cotton fibres become flat and twisted (see chapter on fibres) after the cotton boll has been gathered and, under normal conditions they remain in this state. Cotton fabric made from these flat fibres has a naturally dull surface. In 1850 John Mercer discovered that if the fibres are passed through a strong solution of caustic soda (an alkali, which does not weaken the fibres) they swell up and become round tubes once more and shrink in length. After the caustic soda has been washed off the fibres remain swollen, round and smooth, never becoming flat and twisted again. Later it was found that if these smooth fibres were stretched while the soda was being washed off, they became lustrous, giving a sheen to fabric made from them. Cotton treated in this way is called *mercerized cotton.* It is a rather expensive process but is widely used today because of the attractive appearance it gives. Poplin is one example and mercerized sewing and embroidery threads are others.

Mercerized Cotton
Microscopic diagram

## Permanently Stiffened Fabrics

Fabrics can be stiffened in several ways:
1) By treating with resin.
2) By treating with resin and starch, though this method is not so permanent because starch washes out.

3) By treating with a cellulose solution and acid.

4) If the material is woven with one cotton and one acetate thread alternately in both the warp and the weft and is then pressed with heat the acetate yarn will melt into a sticky substance which will fill up the spaces between the weaving and bind the cotton together. When it has cooled and set, a permanently stiffened material is the result and this is known as Trubenized material. It is used for making stiff collars for shirts.

### Giving Warmth to Fabrics

One way of making materials warmer is to give them a fluffy surface, because the fluffiness entraps air to act as an insulator, thus making a naturally cool material warmer to wear. The material is passed between rollers with a brushing action. The rollers are covered with teazles or fine wire points which brush or fluff up the surface of the fabric. Cotton, viscose and knitted nylon can be brushed to make them slightly warmer. If this treatment is given to woollen fabric when it is dry an upright pile is produced which traps air for warmth as in fabric made for blankets. If woollen fabric is brushed when it is wet the pile is 'laid' as in face cloth.

Milium is a lining material coated with a thin layer of aluminium which acts as an insulator reflecting warmth back into the body in the winter and deflecting the sun's rays in the summer so that it is warm to wear in the winter and cool in the summer. It can be dry-cleaned without harming the finish.

### Milled Woollen Cloth

Worsted cloth does not usually require a finishing process after weaving to improve its appearance but some woollen fabrics do because the yarn is hairy, making the weave looser and more sack-like. It goes through a process known as milling. The fabric is put through a warm, soapy solution in which it is pressed and rubbed so that the fibres felt and thicken and the spaces between the threads close up. The fabric becomes dense and smooth and sometimes the weaving structure does not show at all. Billiard cloths, Melton cloths and flannels are finished in this way.

### Crease-resisting Finishes

Animal fibres do not crease so readily as cottons and rayons and when they do crease they recover more quickly, therefore they do not need anti-crease treatment.

Synthetic resin is introduced right inside the fibres of cottons and rayons and this makes them more resilient and less likely to crease. Therefore resin serves two purposes, making fabric both shrink-resistant and crease-shedding.

### Shrink-resisting Finishes

During the manufacture of material yarn is pulled out and stretched and when it is washed it absorbs moisture and swells so that it becomes larger in diameter and consequently shorter in length, going back to its original size and causing the material to shrink. The spaces between the weaving or knitting close up. There are several treatments which can be used to prevent this happening. One method is to steam the material to close up the fibres without shrinking them and then to set them by pressing them with heat. Another way is to treat the fibres with synthetic resin so that they will not swell up when wetted.

Cotton, linen and some man-made fabrics are treated in these ways.

Lightweight woollen fabrics are treated with various chemicals, then they are steamed ('blown' is the technical term) for a few minutes and finally dried without stretching. This treatment removes the felting properties of wool and prevents shrinkage. Fabrics so treated can be washed and drip-dried and require little ironing. 'Dylan' is a trade name for such a shrink-resist finish.

### Durable Pleating

When the fabrics are made from thermoplastic yarns, polyamides, polyesters and acetate, the pleats are set in with heat and moisture. Nowadays most woollen fabrics can also be durably pleated. First of all the fabric has to be made shrink-resistant and then the pleating is carried out in one of two ways.
a) The entire cloth is impregnated with chemicals so that the pleats can be set in where required by pressing under a damp cloth.
b) A chemical is sprayed onto the part to be creased (such as a trouser crease), which is then pressed and dried.

### Stain-and Water-repellent Finishes

1) Material can be woven so closely from cotton yarn that the fibres swell when wetted and fill up the spaces between them allowing no more water to pass through them.
2) Woollen fabrics can be made showerproof in the following ways: a) Wax is emulsified into small globules and mixed with aluminium acetate and a protein (casein). This substance is then mixed with water; the woollen fabric is dipped into it and then mangled to remove the excess water. The fabric is dried and as the water evaporates the wax is left in the cloth making it showerproof.
b) Silicones are emulsified in water or a solvent and the fabric is immersed in the solution. It is then dried and heated for a few minutes to 140°C when the silicones form a polymer which becomes bonded to the wool, making it very water-repellent.

These methods are not always proof against dry-cleaning but garments can be re-textured by adding wax in a solvent to the cleaning fluid.

Stain resistance can be given by treating woollen cloth with chemicals such as Mystolene MK3 or Scotchguard FC208. It is claimed that dry-cleaning does not destroy these finishes.

### Flameproofing

Some fibres are highly inflammable or flammable, both words meaning the same thing today. These are cottons, linens, viscose, acetate and acrylics. Cotton net, flannelette and winceyette are very inflammable fabrics. Winceyette, because it is cheap, hardwearing and warm is frequently used for children's nightwear. This is most dangerous for if the material comes in contact with an unguarded fire, it will go up in a sheet of flame. Many fatal accidents have been caused in this way. The same thing can happen with party dresses made from cotton net. Cotton, viscose and acetate can be chemically treated by a process known as Pyrovatex to make them flame-resistant. The process will make the material a little stiffer and possibly a little harsher and adds slightly to the cost, but this is of small account compared with the safety it gives. Washing instructions supplied with fabric so treated should be followed very carefully for it is useless if incorrect laundering destroys the finish. Soap, particularly in hard water, can build up in the fabric and become most inflammable, so it is safer to use synthetic detergents.

### Mothproofing

Woollens are the fabrics most likely to be attacked by moth grubs and they can be protected from attack in the following ways:

a) An insecticide called Deilmoth can be dissolved in oil, a solvent or water and applied to the wool yarn during spinning or in dry cleaning fluids. It can also be sprayed on to articles and clothes. It will wash out, but as so very little is needed to mothproof the wool, much more than is necessary is used so that it will survive many washings.

b) A compound called Mitin FF, which is a colourless dye, is mixed in the dye bath when fabric is coloured and mothproofs the fabric for life.

### Finishes which can be applied to Non-Thermoplastic Fabrics

*Cotton.* Shrink-resist, stain-and mildew-resist, flame-resist, water-repellent, glazed, embossed, minimum-care, drip-dry.

*Linen.* Crease-resist, stain-and mildew-resist, water-repellent.

*Wool.* Felting, water-repellent, mothproofing, shrink-resist, semi-permanent pleating, stain-repellent.

*Silk.* Crease-resist.

*Viscose.* Crease-resist, stain-resist, shrink-resist, flame-resistance, water-repellent.

**Finishes which can be applied to Thermoplastic Fabrics**

*Acetate.* Embossing, moire, crease-resist, permanent pleating, flame-resistance.
*Nylon.* Brushed.
*Polyester.* Permanent-pleating, water-repellent, permanent stiffening.
*Permanent Press Koraton treatment.* Garments which have been made up can be treated with resin and then baked into shape.

# 6 A Variety of Fabrics and their uses

A fabric has to stand up reasonably well to the kind of wear and tear it is likely to have to undergo according to the purpose for which it is used. Today we use fabrics for so many pruposes and, of course, some are more suitable for one purpose than for another. Much research is carried out to produce textiles which will have the qualities necessary for the uses for which they are intended.

## QUALITIES

### The Qualities Needed for Fabrics for Work Clothes

1) They must be dense enough to protect the clothes which they cover.
2) They should be resistant to stains, dirt and chemicals. Various finishes which are given to some fabrics help in this respect. Fabrics with smooth, shiny surfaces are less likely to pick up dirt and this is one reason why nylon and polyester are used for overalls.
3) They should be strong and hardwearing and able to stand up to repeated washing and boiling, if necessary.
4) They should not be harmed by dry-cleaning and laundry agents which may have to be used to remove paint, grease and other stains.
5) They should be absorbent and good conductors of heat. This is essential for occupations which are carried out in hot or steamy atmospheres, for example cooking.

### Qualities Needed in Fabrics for Active Sports Clothes

1) They should be absorbent and good conductors of heat owing to the perspiration which we lose during exercise.
2) They must be easily washable.
3) They should be fairly hardwearing and elastic enough to allow for easy movement. In this respect some knitted fabrics are most useful and suitable.
4) They should be an appropriate colour, for instance white for tennis and cricket clothes, coloured and gaily patterned for beachwear and so on.

### Qualities Needed in Fabrics for Children's Clothes

1) They should be as light in weight as possible because heavy clothes are tiring, especially for small children.
2) They must be very strong, hardwearing and elastic as children are extremely

active and, more often than not, have little consideration for their clothes.
3) They must be shrink-resistant and must be able to stand up to constant washing.
4) They should be colourful and attractive to the child.
5) They should be NON-INFLAMMABLE. Many fatal accidents happen because children are dressed in fabrics which will flare up immediately they come in contact with an unguarded fire. This fact cannot be stressed too much.
6) They should be absorbent for comfort, good conductors of heat for summer wear and good insulators for colder weather.

## Qualities Needed in Fabrics for Adult Day Dresses

1) They should be suitable in design, colour, weight and texture for the occasions for which they are to be worn.
2) They should give reasonable wear, bearing in mind the fact that fashions change and have only a limited life. Therefore it is not always necessary for the fabric to outlive the fashion.
3) They must be washable or able to be dry-cleaned without undue trouble or expense.

*Exercise.* Select fabrics suitable for day wear for *(a)* a typist, *(b)* a housewife, *(c)* a cookery teacher, *(d)* a school leaver attending an interview for training as a model.

## Qualities Needed in Fabrics for Evening Clothes

1) The fabrics should be attractive and even glamorous in texture, colour and design.
2) For dancing, which is strenuous, they should be good conductors of heat and absorbent.
3) They should be non-inflammable because dresses are often full and flimsy and come accidentally in contact with radiators.
4) They should have good draping qualities, whether they are stiff, soft or flimsy.
5) Fabrics for wraps and capes and stoles need to be able to hold pockets of air for warmth.

## Qualities Needed in Fabrics for Lingerie

1) They should be lightweight and elastic to allow for movement.
2) They should feel very pleasant against the skin, and be non-irritating.
3) They should be able to absorb perspiration and allow it to evaporate.
4) If possible a deodorant treatment is desirable.
5) They must stand up to frequent washing and be quick to dry.

6) For stiff underslips the fabric should have a permanent stiffness which will withstand washing.

7) An anti-static treatment is desirable for fabrics which pick up and hold dirt.

8) Fabrics should be resistant to abrasion caused by the friction of one garment rubbing on another.

9) For colder weather warmth and lightness are required and here bulked yarns are very suitable.

## Qualities Needed in Fabrics for Travel Wear

1) Lightness in weight is particularly important for air travel where luggage weight is limited.

2) Crease-resistance is vital when garments have to be packed.

3) Easy washing and quick drying.

## Qualities Needed in Fabrics for Wet Weather Clothes

1) They should have a close weave through which water does not penetrate easily.

2) They should be non-absorbent.

3) The yarn in the fabric should be able to swell with moisture and so close up the spaces between the threads making the fabric dense.

4) The fabric should be hairy so that raindrops hang on the hairs without penetrating the fabric.

5) Fabrics should be treated with a showerproof finish.

## Qualities Needed in Fabrics for Interlinings and Underlinings

1) They must be firm enough to hold the shape of such parts of a garment as lapels.

2) They should be lightweight and thin for stiffening collars and cuffs.

3) They should be transparent and featherweight when required for such delicate outer fabrics as lace.

4) They must be of woven fabric when it is necessary to cut on the cross for parts which have to be shaped or which have to give with the grain of the outer material and with movements of the body.

5) They can be of non-woven fabric when needed to counteract stretch in the garment fabric where no such stretch is desired.

6) Fabrics must be crease-shedding to give a smooth, invisible foundation.

7) Underlinings can be fusible to give body to a stretchy outer fabric to help it to retain its shape. Use fusible knitted underlining for knitted fabrics.

8) If an interlining is required to contribute warmth it must be flexible and

lightweight and not too bulky; a man-made fibre wadding, perhaps, or thin foam.
9) It must have the same shrinkage rate as the garment.

## Qualities Needed for Fabrics for Linings

1) They must be thin and lightweight, adding minimum bulk.
2) They must be strong and hardwearing to resist abrasion.
3) They must be slippery so that the garment is easy to get into and does not stick to other clothes.
4) They must have the same rate of shrinkage as the outer fabric.
5) Linings for thermoplastic fabrics MUST be anti-static.
6) The lining must be knitted if the outer fabric is knitted, so that both fabrics will have the same amount of 'give'.

## Qualities Needed in Fabrics for Household Uses

*Curtains*

1) Colours should be fadeless and fast to sunlight.
2) Fabrics should be strong and not rotted by sun.
3) In cold weather the fabric should be heavy enough to keep out draughts and yet allow air to penetrate into a room.
4) They should drape and hang well.

*Upholstery*

1) Fabrics should be strong and resist abrasion because they are subject to constant friction when sat upon.
2) They should be dirt-repellent and easily cleanable. Here fabric-backed plastics are useful as they merely need wiping down.

*Bed linen*

1) Fabrics must stand up to friction caused by movement during sleep.
2) They must be able to absorb perspiration given off by the body.
3) They should be as lightweight as possible. Blanket fabrics must be able to hold pockets of air for warmth.
4) Fabrics should be easily washable.
5) Pillow tickings and eiderdown coverings must be so closely woven that feathers cannot work through them.

*Towels*

1) They must be strong when wet and able to stand up to friction.
2) A mildew-resist treatment will help to protect cottons and linens from being attacked by mildew when they are damp.

3) Fabrics must stand up to boiling so that they can be sterilized.
4) Fabrics for tea towels and glass cloths must be smooth and not shed any fluff.

## COTTON FABRICS

### Cotton for Clothes

**Batiste.** A fabric made from fine yarn in a plain rib weave. It may be white, dyed or embroidered. Used for corsets and brassieres.

**Calico.** This fabric was originally made in Calicut, India, from whence it derived its name. It is a plainly woven, medium weight material which may be unbleached, bleached, dyed or printed. It is usually slightly stiffened with a dressing which washes out. It is used for overalls and uniforms.

**Cambric.** A fine lightweight material originally made in Cambrai, France. It has a slight dressing and is usually calendered which gives it a lustre on one side only. Both the dressing and the lustre wash out. Used for dainty caps and aprons, handkerchiefs and lingerie.

**Corduroy.** A hardwearing material with ribs raised in a pile running down the length of the fabric. The ribs are shaped after weaving and may vary in width. The fabric is dyed after weaving. Used for slacks, skirts, suits and riding breeches.

**Denim.** A strong hardwearing fabric in a twill weave having a coloured warp and a white weft which gives it a slight overall white haze effect. Used for dungarees, jeans, overalls and sportswear.

**Dimity.** A sheer, crisp, fabric with a soft lustre woven from mercerized yarn. It has a thicker thread woven in to make either corded lengthwise stripes or checks. It may be bleached, dyed or printed. Used for children's dresses, blouses and lingerie.

**Drill.** A strong material closely woven with a right to left twill weave. Used for overalls, work uniforms and slacks.

**Flannelette.** A soft fabric in either a plain or twill weave. The surface is brushed up to give it a fluffy nap, making a naturally cool fabric warmer to wear. It is highly inflammable unless given a flame-resist finish. Used for children's nightwear.

**Gabardine.** Can be made entirely from cotton, entirely from wool or from a mixture of both. The fabric is closely woven in a twill weave showing on the surface only. It is often treated to make it showerproof for raincoats. It can be used for slacks, suits and skirts.

**Gingham.** A lightweight fabric which may be woven with coloured yarns in striped or check patterns or in plain colours. It wears and washes well. Used for children's summer dresses and for aprons.

**Lawn.** A very light fabric woven from fine yarn in a plain weave. It can be bleached, dyed or printed. Sometimes it is slightly starched. Used for blouses, lingerie and baby clothes.

**Lace** All over lace fabric made from cotton can be used for dresses and underwear. Lace edgings in various widths and patterns are made for trimmings.

**Muslin.** A very fine material loosely woven. Used for blouses, babies' and children's dresses.

**Nainsook.** A light soft material in a plain weave made from mercerized yarn. It can be calendered to give it an extra gloss on one side. Used for lingerie and babies' clothes.

**Net.** An open mesh fabric, highly inflammable unless flame-resist treated. Used for party dresses, frilly petticoats and for trimming for lingerie.

**Organdie.** A sheer, crisp, transparent material tightly woven in a plain weave from very fine yarn. It is dyed in delicate colours and may be printed, flock printed or embroidered. It is treated chemically to give it a permanent crispness. Used for blouses, children's and babies' dresses, pram pillow-slips, dainty embroidered tray-cloths and table cloths. It is also used as an interlining for collars and cuffs in blouses and lightweight dresses.

**Piqué.** A firm, medium weight fabric with a raised surface in either a Bedford cord rib or honeycomb weave, known as waffle piqué. It may be bleached, dyed or printed. It is strong and hardwearing. Used for blouses, summer dresses and sportswear and for accessories such as collars and cuffs.

**Plissé.** A lightweight fabric with a permanent puckered stripe or pattern produced after weaving by one of the following methods:
1) The stripe or pattern is printed on to the fabric with strong caustic soda. It is then steamed and the printed parts shrink, causing the unprinted parts to pucker.
2) The stripes are printed with a substance which resists caustic soda. The fabric is then put into a caustic soda solution and the unprinted parts shrink.
Used for lingerie and summer dresses and blouses.

**Poplin.** A material made from mercerized yarn in a fine ribbed weave. The weave is in fact plain and the rib is formed by using a weft yarn which is thicker than the warp. The fabric is of medium weight and has a soft sheen. It is hardwearing and washes well. It can have a drip-dry finish. It is used for dresses, blouses, sportswear, shirts, and light-weight coats.

**Repp.** A firm material in which heavy weft threads form distinct ribs running across it. Lighter weight repps are used for dresses and suits and summer coats.

**Sail-cloth.** A very strong, firm, canvas-type fabric made in various weights. May be dyed or printed. Not originally intended for a clothing fabric but nowadays the lighter weights are used for jeans, sportswear and even summer dresses and skirts.

**Seersucker.** A lightweight fabric with puckered lengthwise stripes resembling plissé, the difference being that, in this case, the stripes are produced during the weaving by arranging groups of warp threads alternately tight and loose. It is used for summer dresses, blouses, pyjamas and nightdresses.

**Terry Towelling.** A fabric with shaggy loops all over the surface. It may be white, dyed, yarn dyed or printed. Used for babies' nappies and beachwear.

**Tobralco.** A lightweight fabric in a haircord weave giving it a very finely ribbed surface, the ribs running lengthwise. It may be bleached, dyed and printed. It wears and washes very well. Used for summer dresses and blouses and children's wear.

**Velveteen.** This material has a cotton base with a short, closely set, woven-in pile which may be made from mercerized cotton or rayon. Used for dresses, skirts, children's coats and for trimmings on collars and cuffs.

**Voile.** A sheer muslin-like material made from tightly twisted yarn. Sometimes it has raised dots woven into it at intervals, or it can have drawn threads or be embroidered. Suitable for dainty blouses and dresses.

**Winceyette.** A soft, warm, hardwearing fabric with a fluffed-up surface similar to flannelette. Highly inflammable unless given flame-resist treatment. Used for children's nightwear although really very dangerous for this purpose unless treated.

### Cottons for Stiffenings and Interlinings

**Buckram.** A loosely woven fabric, sized with glue to make it stiff. Does not remain stiff after washing. Used for interlinings, hat shapes or moulds and for bookbinding.

**Staflex.** An interlining for collars and cuffs, etc., with one adhesive surface which can be ironed on to the garment to hold it permanently in place. Made in two qualities, one suitable for dry-cleaning and the other for washing. It can be either woven or knitted.

**Tarlatan.** A transparent loosely woven muslin which is given a dressing to stiffen it. Used for petticoats to make dresses stand away from the figure.

### Cottons for Household Uses

**Balloon Fabrics.** Very closely woven from fine cotton yarn in a plain weave. Can be used for lightweight downproof interlinings for cushions.

**Bedford cord.** The name is given to the weave as well as to the fabric. It has a lengthwise rib which can vary in width. Used for upholstery.

**Brocade.** Brocade has a pattern woven into it. The cotton yarn may be woven with other yarns, such as rayons, to produce a silky pattern on a dull background, or the other way about. Used for curtains, loose covers, etc.

**Calico.** See under cottons for clothes. Used for under pillow-slips, ironing-board covers and so on.

**Candlewick.** Thick yarn in tufts is worked into a woven base. Then the base fabric is shrunk and holds the tufts permanently in place. Used for bathmats and bedspreads.

# COTTON FABRICS

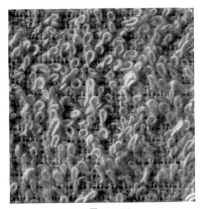

Terry Towelling

Ticking

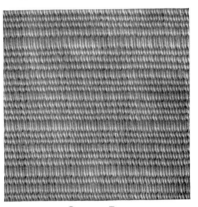

Cotton Repp

Sateen

All micro-photographs are slightly enlarged

# COTTON FABRICS

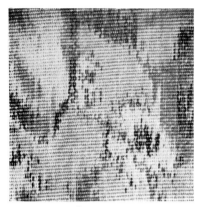

Cretonne

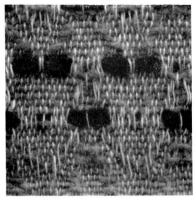

Folk Weave

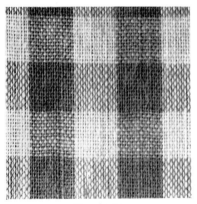

Gingham

Corduroy

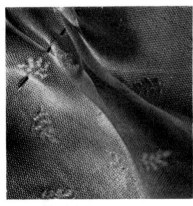

Flock Printed Organdie

Needlecord

# COTTON FABRICS

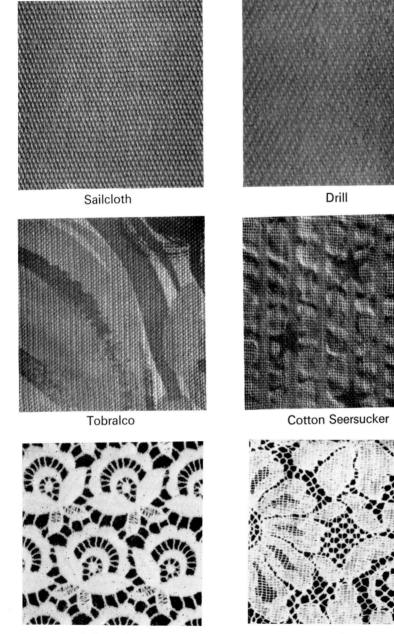

Sailcloth

Drill

Tobralco

Cotton Seersucker

Guipure Lace

Leavers Lace

# COTTON FABRICS

Bincarette                    Piqué

## LINEN FABRICS

Damask Linen              Embroidery Linen

Huckaback                 Even Weave Linen

# WOOL FABRICS

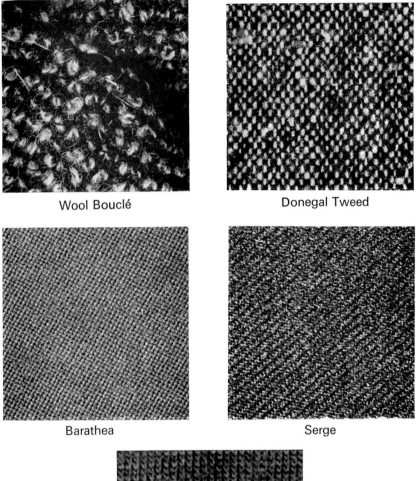

Wool Bouclé

Donegal Tweed

Barathea

Serge

Wool Jersey

# SILK FABRICS

Satin

Chiffon

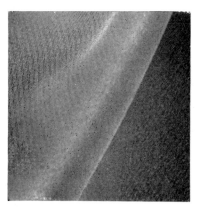

Crêpe de Chine

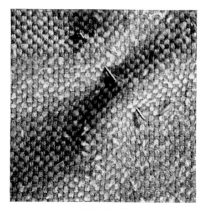

Silk Noil

Velvet

Slub Weave Viscose

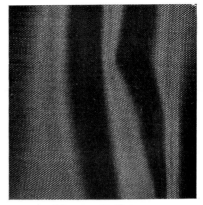

Viscose Taffeta

Viscose Brocade

Embossed Acetate

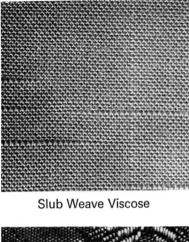

Brushed Nylon

Nylon Plissé

# MAN-MADE FIBRES

Nylon Fur Fabric

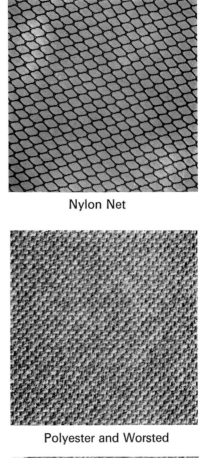

Nylon Net

Polyester Curtain Net

Polyester and Worsted

Courtelle Jersey

Fibreglass

**Casement cloth.** A medium-weight fabric in a closely woven plain weave. Usually dyed in plain colours. Used for light curtains.

**Chintz.** A glazed fabric, usually with a pattern printed on it. The glaze may be produced by treating the fabric with starch or wax and then pressing with hot rollers. This type of glaze washes out, but nowadays the fabric can be treated chemically to produce a glaze which will withstand washing and be permanent. Used for curtains, eiderdown covers, cushion covers, etc.

**Crash.** A fabric in a plain weave rather loosely woven in coarse yarn. Used for embroidery for chair backs, cushion covers, table runners, etc.

**Cretonne.** A firmly woven fabric in a plain weave, rather like chintz but not glazed. Often printed with patterns which have a shadowy outline. This is caused by printing the pattern on to the warp threads only and then weaving in the weft with white yarn. The fabric is often reversible. Used for curtains, cushion covers and loose covers for settees and chairs.

**Damask.** A damask fabric has the pattern permanently woven into it. Usually a matt pattern on a satin weave background which is reversed on the underside. Used for table linen.

**Flannelette.** See under cottons for clothes. Used for flannelette sheets.

**Folkweave.** A soft furnishing fabric made from coarse yarn loosely woven, often in striped patterns. The colours are not always fast and are inclined to run when washed. Used for curtains and bedspreads.

**Gingham.** See under cottons for clothes. Used for light curtains.

**Java canvas.** A fabric for embroidery, woven with distinct squares in a basket weave, very easy to count for cross stitch and suitable for use with the heavier kinds of embroidery thread.

**Lace.** All over cotton lace is used for curtains.

**Muslin.** See under cottons for clothes. Often used for dainty curtains.

**Repp.** See under cottons for clothes. The heavier types are used for upholstery and furnishings.

**Sateen.** A strong lightweight fabric with a satin weave running across it. It has a glossy sheen on one side only. It can be treated to make it downproof and is used for the underside of eiderdowns because of its light weight. Also used for curtain linings.

**Terry Towelling.** See under cottons for clothes. Used for bath and hand towels, face flannels, roller towels and tea towels.

**Ticking.** A strong fabric very closely woven in twill, herringbone or satin weaves. It can have a damask pattern on it and it can be woven in stripes with coloured yarn. Used for mattress covers, pillow ticks and upholstery.

**Velveteen.** See under cottons for clothes. The heavier types are used for cushion covers, curtains and upholstery.

### Cottons for Outdoor Use

**Awning.** Made from coarse yarn in a close plain weave. The yarn is sometimes dyed and woven in stripes. Used for sunblinds, awnings and hammocks.

**Bunting.** A plainly woven material usually dyed in bright colours which are seldom fast to sunlight or washing. Used mainly for flags and for decorating bazaar stalls.

**Canvas.** A coarse fabric made from coarse yarn in a plain weave. It can be made in various weights and the yarn can be dyed and woven in stripes. Used for upholstery covers, deck-chairs, etc.

**Cotton duck.** A heavyweight type of canvas, closely woven and very strong. It can be dyed or printed. Used for awnings and for covering furniture.

**Sail-cloth.** See under cottons for clothes. Heavy type is used for sails.

## LINEN FABRICS

### Linens for Clothes

**Cambric.** See under cotton. This fabric can also be made from very fine linen yarn and is more expensive than the cotton variety.

**Dress Linen.** There are many fabrics made from linen yarn, usually plainly woven, intended for summer dresses and women's suits. Moygashel linens being examples. They are made in various weights and can be dyed and printed.

**Drill.** Linen drill is a firm cool fabric in a fine twill weave. It is used for men's tropical suits.

**Lawn.** Linen lawn is a very fine fabric in a plain weave. It is strong, soft and absorbent. Used for making dainty embroidered blouses and handkerchiefs.

**Tailor's canvas.** An unbleached coarse fabric in a plain weave used for interlining the collars and revers of coats.

### Linens for Household Uses

**Brocade.** A heavy fabric in a jacquard weave, strong and hardwearing. Beautiful patterns are woven in various colours. The fabric hangs and drapes well and is suitable for curtains and upholstery.

**Crash Towelling.** A strong absorbent fabric in a plain weave, suitable for roller towels.

**Damask.** Fabric in a jacquard weave with a damask pattern (see under cottons). It is very smooth and has a beautiful sheen and is used for good quality table linen.

**Glass cloth fabric.** A smooth fabric in a plain weave, sometimes woven in stripes with coloured yarn. It is absorbent and in no way fluffy and therefore is suitable for glass cloths and tea towels.

**Huckaback.** A towelling fabric in a huckaback weave which produces a slightly raised pattern on both surfaces. It is strong and absorbent and is used for hand towels and guest towels.

**Sheeting.** A fabric in a close plain weave, very strong and cool. Used for sheets and pillow-slips.

**Terry Towelling.** See under cottons. Linen terry towelling is very strong and slightly harsh compared with the cotton fabric. It is also more expensive.

**Ticking.** A strong, very closely woven fabric in a herringbone weave. Used for mattress covers and pillow-ticks.

### Linens for Outdoor Uses

**Awning.** A strong heavy fabric in a plain weave woven in stripes with coloured yarn. Used for awnings.

**Flax Duck.** A very heavy type of canvas used for tents.

**Tarpaulin.** Extremely heavy fabric, sometimes given waterproof treatment. Used for covering lorries and for agricultural purposes.

### Linens for Embroidery

**Art Linens.** There are a variety of fabrics woven from linen for embroidery purposes in various weights, widths and colours. Examples are 'Old Bleach' and 'Glenshee' linens. As linen yarn is naturally uneven, being thicker in some places than in others, these fabrics are expensive because they are made from even yarn. The weave has to be even to make the fabric suitable for drawn and counted threadwork otherwise the embroidery stitches would be of varying size. The fabrics are coarse or fine according to the thickness of the yarn used to weave them. Some may have only seven threads to the square centimetre each way while others have as many as eleven or more.

**Tapestry canvas.** A canvas in an open weave made especially for tapestry work.

## SILK FABRICS

### Silks for Clothes

**Brocade.** Stiff fabric woven in a pattern in a jacquard weave. Used for evening dresses.

**Chiffon.** A sheer material in an open plain weave. Very light, filmy and soft. Used for blouses, evening dresses, very delicate lingerie.

**Crêpe de Chine.** A lightweight fabric with a smooth surface woven plainly from two types of silk yarn. A flat yarn is used for the warp and a crinkled or crêpe one for the weft. The fabric has a soft sheen and drapes beautifully. Suitable for dresses, blouses and lingerie.

**Faille.** A fabric with a fine lengthwise rib. Used for dresses, coats and suits.

**Foulard.** A lightweight material with a twill weave. Usually it has a printed pattern and is used for dresses.

**Georgette.** A sheer material in a plain loose weave. A little heavier than chiffon and it has a crêpe surface because crêpe yarn is used for both the warp and the weft. Used for blouses, evening dresses and for flimsy lingerie.

**Grosgrain.** A closely woven material with ribs running across. Used for suits and for ribbons.

**Jap Silk.** A very light, closely woven, fine fabric made from nett silk in a plain weave. It is not weighted. Used for linings mostly.

**Lace.** All over lace is used for evening dresses and lingerie.

**Milanese.** A knitted fabric suitable for lingerie.

**Net.** Open mesh fabric used for evening dresses and petticoats.

**Ninon.** A sheer fabric woven in a plain weave with twisted yarn. A little stiffer and a little heavier than chiffon. Used for scarves and filmy evening dresses.

**Organza.** A sheer material resembling cotton organdie. Used for evening dresses.

**Ottoman.** A heavy fabric with distinct ribs running across it. Used for coats and suits.

**Pongee.** A material made from wild silk in a plain weave. The yarn is irregular being thicker in places than in others and this produces a slightly slubbed effect in the fabric. It is a natural ecru colour or it may be dyed. It is woven in 'the gum', which is washed out afterwards. Used for blouses, dresses and underwear.

**Poult.** A stiffish material in a plain weave. The weft threads are thicker than the warp and this produces a ribbed effect. Used for evening dresses.

**Shantung.** A fabric woven plainly with irregular wild silk yarn. It has a slubbed effect. Can be a natural ecru colour, dyed or printed. It is woven in 'the gum' which is removed later. It is slightly crisp to handle and has a soft lustre. Suitable for dresses, blouses, housecoats and dressing-gowns.

**Slipper Satin.** A beautiful fabric with a satin surface and a ribbed underside. (Satin beauté has a crêpe underside). Used for evening dresses and lingerie.

**Spun Silk.** This material is made from yarn spun from the short lengths of silk which cannot be reeled. The weave is plain and even and the fabric has not quite such a lustrous sheen as those woven with nett silk. Used for dresses and blouses.

**Suzette.** A sheer crêpe material suitable for lingerie.

**Taffeta.** A crisp, slightly stiff fabric in a plain weave with a thicker weft than warp yarn, giving a slightly ribbed effect. Shot taffeta is woven with the warp in one colour and the weft in another. The material is usually weighted. Used for evening dresses, petticoats and linings.

**Tussore.** A lightweight crisp material woven plainly from wild silk in 'the gum'. Ecru coloured or dyed or printed. Suitable for blouses and dresses.

**Velvet.** A fabric with a woven-in pile. Chiffon velvet is light in weight and has a beautiful soft sheen. It drapes well and catches the light on the folds. Usually dyed in plain colours. It can have a pattern embossed on it with rollers. Panne velvet has a pile pressed in one direction. In brocaded velvet the pile is removed from the background with chemicals so that only the pattern stands out. Used for evening dresses and wraps and for suits, hats and trimmings.

### Silks for Household Uses

**Brocade.** The heavier types of silk brocade are used for curtains, cushion covers and upholstery.
**Crêpe de Chine.** This can be used for covering eiderdowns and for bedspreads.
**Organza.** Suitable for very light curtains.
**Taffeta.** Used for eiderdown covers and bedspreads.
**Velvet.** Can be used for curtains and upholstery.

## SOME WOOLLEN FABRICS

### Woollens for Clothes

**Alpaca.** In this fabric the warp is cotton and the weft is yarn obtained from alpaca goats' hair. It may have a twill or plain weave. Used for men's light jackets.
**Angora.** Materials made from either angora rabbits' or angora goats' hair, in various weights suitable for dresses and coats.
**Astrakhan.** This is a fabric made to resemble astrakhan fur. It is woven from woollen, mohair or viscose yarns which have been curled. Used for winter coats, hats and trimmings.
**Barathea.** A fabric made from worsted yarns in a twill weave. It is of medium weight and has a smooth surface. Usually dyed in plain colours. Used for suits, jacket dresses and dresses.
**Bouclé.** A bouclé material is woven with yarns which have been looped. The fabric has a knobbled texture and the warp and weft can be of different colours. It is made in various weights suitable for dresses, suits and coats.
**Cavalry Twill.** A firm fabric with a left to right twill weave. Dyed in plain colours. Used for coats, suits and slacks.
**Donegal Tweed.** A tweed made from hairy yarn which has various coloured specks in it here and there. The lighter weights are suitable for dresses and skirts and the heavier types for sports jackets and men's suits.
**Felt.** A bonded fabric made from short wool fibres lying in all directions, which become interlocked with steam, heat and pressure into a dense material. Dyed in plain, clear colours. Used for skirts, bonnets, gloves and belts.
**Flannel.** Can be a light weight with an open plain weave suitable for babies' clothes or it can be a heavy weight in a plain or twill weave for suits, slacks and blazers. Union flannel is á mixture of wool and cotton.

**Gabardine.** See under cotton. Wool gabardine is often used for raincoats because, even without showerproof treatment, it is naturally water-repellent. Also used for light coats and suits.

**Jersey.** A knitted fabric which drapes softly and is elastic and comfortable to wear. Usually dyed in plain colours but can be printed and is often knitted with coloured yarns in patterns. Used for dresses, skirts and light jersey suits.

**Nuns' Veiling.** A very lightweight fabric which is soft and firm. Woven with twisted yarn and dyed in plain colours or bleached. Suitable for children's dresses.

**Serge.** A medium weight, rather wiry fabric with a distinct, smooth twill weave. Usually dyed in plain colours. Used for skirts, gym tunics and trousers and suits.

**Tweed.** A harsh, hairy fabric in various weaves — plain, twill or herringbone. Plain colours or woven-in patterns — checks, stripes, tartans, dog's tooth, etc., with coloured yarn. Lightweights are used for dresses and skirts and the heavier types for coats, suits and jackets.

**Velour.** Heavy fabric woven in a satin or twill weave with a short pile. The nap runs in one direction. Used for coats and dresses.

**Viyella.** Pre-shrunk, lightweight fabric, plain or printed, for dresses and children's clothes.

**Wool Crêpe de Chine and Georgette.** Lightweight fabrics made from crêpe yarns for blouses and dresses.

### Woollens for Household Uses

**Carpeting.** Many types of carpet are made with woollen fibres. They may be woven, as some rugs are, or they may have a velvet type of pile.

**Blankets.** Woven in a plain weave from fairly thick yarn, sometimes with coloured yarn woven in to form stripes. They may be dyed in plain colours.

**Felt.** Heavy felt is used for carpets and surrounds and for underlays for ironing-boards and tables.

**Plush.** A velour fabric with a heavy pile. Used for curtains, upholstery and table covers.

### MAN-MADE FIBRES

Today the man-made fibres are used to make almost every kind of fabric which was originally made from cotton, linen, wool, silk, fur or leather. They are often blended with the natural fibres to provide qualities which these fibres lack. In fact more man-made fibre is now being used than cotton in the British Textile Industry.

If a fabric made of synthetic fibre is given the name of the original fabric made from natural fibre, the name of the synthetic fibre should precede the name of the fabric, for example, *organza* is a fabric made from silk but, when it is made from viscose it should be called *viscose organza* to distinguish it from silk. Jersey fabrics are almost always preceded by the name of the fibre, wool jersey, nylon jersey, polyester jersey, acrylic jersey, etc.

## Synthetic Fabrics Used for Clothing

**Dress Fabrics.** Crêpes, brushed rayons, georgettes, voiles and many lightweight fabrics are made for children's and adults' summer and evening dresses, in plain colours, woven in patterns or printed. Heavier types of fabric resembling wool are made for warmer dresses often from a mixture or blend of fibres. Stretch fabrics are also being used.

**Fur Fabrics.** Fabrics with a deep pile made from polyamide and acrylic fibres. Warm to wear and may be lightweight. Used for coats.

**Lace and Net.** Fabrics suitable for evening wear or as edgings and trimmings.

**Lingerie Fabrics.** These include stretch, woven and lightweight knitted fabrics. Bulked and brushed yarns are used for warmer nightwear.

**Overalls.** Plain nylon and polyester fabrics are very suitable for overalls as they are easily washed and dried, are hardwearing and resistant to chemicals. They may be lightweight or heavy industrial weight, in all colours and are often durably pleated.

**Raincoats.** Close weave nylon and polyester fabrics are used for this purpose when suitably proofed.

**Ribbons.** Nylon and polyester ribbons are made suitable for trimmings and shoulder-straps.

**Shirtings.** Usually drip-dry and non-iron fabrics. Sometimes a plain weave with stripes woven in, sometimes knitted. Made from polyester cotton usually.

**Suitings.** These fabrics are used for men's and women's suits, for durably pleated skirts and for trousers. The synthetic fibre is often blended with wool to make worsted yarns.

## Synthetic Fabrics for Household Uses

**Bedspreads.** Many silky types of fabric are made for bedspreads and household draperies and also Tricel candlewick fabrics.

**Blankets.** Very lightweight, luxurious, fleecy fabrics made from acrylic fibres. Dyed in pleasant, cheerful colours.

**Brocades.** Patterned fabrics in a jacquard weave suitable for upholstery, cushions, curtains, etc.

**Curtain Nets. (Polyester)** These are light open-weave fabrics resembling muslins and cotton nets. Only polyester is used for this purpose as it resists sunlight. (Nylon is rotted by sunlight).

**Damask.** Hardwearing, easily washed fabric used for tablecloths, table napkins. Often coloured.

**Pillow and Eiderdown Filling.** A pure white down-like filling. Very soft, light and warm, mothproof and washable.
**Sheets.** Nylon, polyester and cotton, and Vincel and cotton are popular as they are strong and hardwearing with attractive colouring and patterns, easily washed and quickly dried and do not shrink.

### Fabrics for Interlining

**Bonded Fabrics, e.g. Lantor, and Vilene.** These are trade names for fabrics in which man-made fibres are bonded together with an adhesive to form a novel fabric suitable for interlining collars, cuffs, etc. They are made in different weights for use with light or heavy fabrics. They are often used to line full skirts which are meant to stand away from the figure.
**Fusible interlinings, e.g. Staflex and Vilene.** Fabrics which have one adhesive surface and can be ironed on to the garment fabric and will remain permanently fixed.

### Acrylic Bonded Fabrics

These are quite different bonded fabrics as they are not just interlinings but are made up of the outer fabric, an interlining, which is a layer of foam, and the lining — all three fabrics being fused together into one. The outer fabric may be jersey, tweed, poplin or suedette and the lining is acrylic fleece. These fabrics make very light, warm jackets, coats, raincoats and dressing gowns and have the advantage of being completely washable. Nowadays many fabrics are being bonded to knitted synthetic fabrics such as nylon. Before buying check that the grain of the fabric has not been pulled awry. These fabrics do not need underlining and are easy to handle.

### PLASTIC SHEETINGS

**Plasticised Vinyl Film.** A transparent sheeting made in various weights which can be coloured, embossed, or printed with patterns and which is not really a fabric. It is dense and waterproof and so is used for macintoshes, aprons and toilet bags. It is not very strong and is easily torn. It is affected by the temperature for in warm weather it becomes quite soft and pliable while in cold weather it becomes stiff and crackly. With age it becomes less pliable and may discolour. It can be used for window curtains but is not very hygienic for this purpose because when the curtains are closed, no air can penetrate into the room through them and the atmosphere can become stuffy. As curtains for shower baths it is most suitable. Plastic tablecloths can be wiped clean easily and have their uses.
    Storage bags made from this plastic film are immensely useful as they are completely mothproof if well sealed, provided that the article being stored is

free from moth grubs when it is put into the bag. Hanging wardrobes are another use for plastic sheeting as they are also mothproof and take up little room where space is limited.

When plastic sheeting is backed with fabric it becomes very much stronger and there are varieties which are extremely tough and suitable for upholstery. These are printed in gay and attractive patterns or they may be just a plain colour.

**Plastic Coated Cotton.** Cotton prints coated with transparent plastic are used mostly for rainwear but also make good, strong, mothproof blanket bags for storage purposes. This is much stronger than plastic sheeting by itself.

Gold and silver embossed plastic coated cottons are heavier and are often used for evening skirts and handbags.

# 7 Sewing Fabrics

## COTTON FABRICS

Cotton fabrics are amongst the easiest to handle and sew as they are firm and do not fray greatly on the whole.

### Treatment Before Cutting Out

*Shrinking.* Unless given anti-shrink treatment by the manufacturers cotton fabrics shrink. Therefore it is wise to shrink any which are not pre-shrunk, before cutting out, so that garments and furnishings will not become too small after the first washing. This can be done in one of three ways. (1) Fabrics such as calico, drill and those which are not glazed by calendering can be put into a water bath for two or three hours and then dried and ironed. (2) The fabric can be wrapped up overnight in a sheet or cloth which has been well wrung out of clean water. (3) Fabrics which have been sized to stiffen them or calendered to give them a sheen are best damp pressed because the size and sheen will wash out at the first laundering. To do this soak a pressing cloth in clean water and wring it out well. Place the fabric face down on an ironing-board and put the damp cloth on top of it on the wrong side. Press a hot iron up and down all over it to create a steam. (Do not slide the iron along). Move the pressing cloth until all the fabric has been damp pressed, re-damping the cloth as it becomes dry. Dry the material off with the heat of the iron. Alternatively a steam iron can be used on the wrong side of the fabric. This method does not shrink the material quite so thoroughly as either of the two preceding methods.

*Straightening the grain.* Sometimes during the finishing processes the grain of cotton fabrics becomes slightly wrung. If both ends of the material are torn along a straight thread and it is then folded in half lengthwise with the selvedges parallel, the torn ends do not lie parallel, see diagram. When this happens the grain must be straightened before cutting out. Hold the corners of one end of the material and enlist the help of a friend to hold those of the other end. Pull sharply on opposite corners, that is diagonally, until the torn ends will lie together when the fabric is folded lengthwise.

**Needles and Thread to use**

| Fabric Type | Sewing Thread | Number of Machine Stitches Per cm | Machine Needle Size | | Hand Needle Size |
|---|---|---|---|---|---|
| | | | English | (Continental) | |
| Net and lace. | 80-100 cotton or mercerized cotton. | 6-4 | 9 | (80) | 10-11 |
| Sheer fabrics. Cambrics, lawn, organdie, voile. | 80-100 cotton or mercerized cotton. | 6 | 9 | (80) | 10-11 |
| Medium weight. Calico, poplin dress cottons, shirtings. | 40-60 cotton or mercerized cotton. | 5 | 14 | (90) | 7-8 |
| Heavy weight. Sailcloth, repp, denim, corduroy velveteen, ticking. | 30-40 cotton or mercerized cotton. | 4 | 16 | (100) | 6-7 |
| Very heavy weight. Canvas, cotton duck. | 24-30 cotton. | 3 | 19-21 | (100) | 3-4 |
| Cotton jersey | 50 mercerized cotton. | 5 | 11 | (70) | |
| For embroidery. | Stranded cotton or coton à broder. | | | | Crewel needles. 5-8 according to the number of strands used |

*Cutting out.* When cutting out clothes in cotton fabrics, use sharp scissors and cut with clean, decisive strokes. For curtains and articles requiring straight edges the material can be torn across to get the grain straight. A difficulty may be encountered here when the fabric has a pattern printed on it, because sometimes the pattern is printed a little off the grain, in other words it may be slightly crooked, so that when it is torn across, the pattern of one curtain may not quite match that of the other. In this case the matching of the pattern may have to be sacrificed because the curtains must be cut on the grain in order to hang properly. When the design is small this is not so noticeable, but with large patterns it can be quite conspicuous and irritating.

## LINEN FABRICS

### Preparation Before Cutting Out

1) If necessary straighten the grain by pulling the fabric diagonally.
2) Iron out all creases.
3) When a straight edge is needed, draw a thread out of the fabric and cut along the space it leaves. Most embroidery linens are cut in this way by shop assistants, as it is the most accurate way of measuring up expensive fabric and it is almost impossible to tear linen because the threads are so strong.

### Cutting Out

Some of the heavier dress and embroidery linens fray very badly as soon as they are cut and are best cut out with pinking shears leaving wider turnings than the pattern allows. The pinked edges must be trimmed off later when the seams are neatened. When pieces of linen are to be embroidered they are, of course, handled quite a lot and then it is wise to tack a temporary hem on all cut edges to prevent fraying.

### Making up.

The seams of those linens which fray badly are best neatened with very close overcasting or blanket stitch or, better still, with machine overcasting. Where they occur in unlined jackets the neatest method is to bind the seams with crossway strips of thin lawn.

Always press seams on the wrong side whenever possible as pressing on the the right side may leave shiny impressions.

**Needles and Thread to use**

| Fabric Type | Sewing Thread | Number of Machine Stitches Per cm | Machine Needle Size | | Hand Needle Size |
|---|---|---|---|---|---|
| | | | English | (Continental) | |
| Lawn and fine linens. | 80-100 cotton. | 6 | 9-11 | (70) | 9-10 |
| Dress weight. | 40-60 mercerized cotton. | 5 | 14 | (90) | 8 |
| Suitings. | 40 mercerized cotton. | 4 | 16 | (100) | 8 |
| Heavy canvas. | Linen thread. | 3 | 19 | (100) | 5 |
| Fine embroidery linens. | Stranded cotton. Coton à broder. Pure silk. Very fine wool. | | | | Crewel 1-10 |
| Heavy embroidery linens and open weaves. | As above and also heavier types of cotton silk, wool or rayons. | | | | Chenille and Tapestry No. 19. |

## SILK FABRICS

### Preparation Before Cutting Out

1) Press out all creases with a warm iron.

2) Pin the selvedges together with very fine pins or, better still, with needles, as pins may catch on the fine threads and cause puckering and they may mark the fabric. Place the pins across the selvedges to hold the material firmly in place because if they are put in lengthwise, the top layer of material is pushed along a little on the lower layer and is then out of position, slightly off grain.

3) Do not use more pins than are necessary to hold pattern pieces in place, particularly when cutting out velvets, to prevent undue marking.

### Cutting Out

Use very sharp scissors and cut with long strokes, keeping the fabric absolutely flat on the table.

### Making Up

1) Silk fabrics can be tailor tacked, but on the sheer and fine slippery varieties the fitting line is best traced out with an outline of flat tacking. This is quite the most satisfactory method as tailor tacks are apt to slip out of silky materials and chiffons, ninon and the soft, unweighted silks are difficult to handle and so a complete outline of tacking is the easiest way of ensuring straight seams and a good line. Use silk sewing thread for the tacking as tacking cotton is a little rough and may pull the threads of the fabric. The tacking up of a garment should be carried out as follows: pass the needle over 15 mm of fabric and pick up 3 mm, pass over 15 mm and again pick up 3 mm, continue in this way producing a long and a short stitch alternately. This holds material more firmly than a series of even-sized stitches.

**Needles and Threads to use**

| Fabric Type | Sewing Thread | Number of Machine Stitches Per cm | Machine Needle Size | | Hand Needle Size |
|---|---|---|---|---|---|
| | | | English | (Continental) | |
| Lace and net. | Silk. | 6-8 | 9 | (80) | 10-11 |
| Sheer fabrics. Chiffon, ninon, georgette, organza. | Silk. | 6 | 9 | (80) | 10-11 |
| Lightweight. Jap silk, shantung, tussore. | Silk. | 4 | 14 | (90) | 8 |
| Medium weight. Taffeta, faille, crêpe-de-Chine, satin, gros-grain, foulard, velvet. | Silk. | 4 | 14 | (90) | 8 |
| Heavy. Brocades. | Silk. | 4 | 14 | (90) | 8 |
| Embroidery. | Pure silk embroidery threads | | | | Crewel 1-10 |

2) Always use fine machine and sewing needles because the silk threads are very fine and thick needles would catch them and cause puckering.

3) Always use sewing silk thread for stitching as it is more elastic than other threads and matches the elasticity of the fabric so that seams will not split.

4) Sheer fabrics require careful stitching and the seams should be tacked to tissue paper before machining to prevent puckering.

5) Chiffon velvets should be cut and put together with the pile smoothing upwards to obtain the richest effect.

6) When parts of a garment need interlining organdie is very suitable as it is light, transparent and permanently crisp. For heavier silks, lightweight bonded interlinings can be used.

7) When pressing use a warm iron on the wrong side and NEVER use a damping cloth as this could cause watermarks in some silks, particularly in those made from wild silks such as shantung and tussore.

For velvets use a velvet board or hold the fabric up and pass the iron over the wrong side. Finger marks can be removed by holding the fabric for a few moments in the steam of a boiling kettle.

## WOOL FABRICS

### Preparation Before Cutting Out

1) Woollen fabrics shrink unless they have had shrink-resist treatment. When wool is blended with another fibre such as cotton or polyester it is not liable to shrink so much. Fabrics with a loose open weave will shrink more than the hard, tightly woven ones. When purchasing woollen material hold it up to the light to see how large the spaces are between the threads in the weave. Notice also, the strength and thickness of the weft threads and how much stretch there is in the fabric. If the weft is thin and weak the material may not wear well and if there is much stretch, slim dresses and tight skirts may 'seat' and slacks will 'bag' at the knees.

To be on the safe side all woollen fabrics should be shrunk before cutting out. The most satisfactory way to do this is to open it out and wrap it up overnight in a sheet wrung out of water so that it gets thoroughly damp all over. Then press it dry.

A quicker method is to damp press it. Wring a damping cloth out of water and place it over the wrong side of the woollen fabric. Press a warm iron up and down all over it creating a steam. Lift the cloth and pat the steam away, then dry off with the *heat* and not the pressure of the iron. Repeat this process over the entire surface of the material not missing any of it, otherwise it will shrink unevenly. Be careful not to ripple the selvedges or they will not lie evenly together during cutting out.

**Needles and Thread to use**

| Fabric Type | Sewing Thread | Number of Machine Stitches Per cm | Machine Needle Size | | Hand Needle Size |
|---|---|---|---|---|---|
| | | | English | (Continental) | |
| Lace. | Pure silk. | 6 | 9 | (80) | 10-11 |
| Fine cashmere, nun's veiling, Viyella. | Pure silk. | 5 | 11 | (70) | 8 |
| Medium dress weights, worsted. | Pure silk. | 4 | 14 | (90) | 8 |
| Heavy. Flannels, tweeds, coatings. | Pure silk. | 4 | 14 | (90) | 8 |

**Cutting Out**

This presents little difficulty except with the loosely woven tweeds and bouclés which fray very easily. Use pinking shears for these fabrics, leaving wider turnings to trim off when the seams are neatened.

**Making Up**

1) Fabrics which are spongy, soft or stretchy are likely to 'seat' and not hold their shape during wear. They should be lined throughout to give good results. Wool jersey is always best lined. The 'seating' will, of course, shrink back to its original size if pressed with a warm iron under a damp cloth, but it is a nuisance to have to do this every time the garment is worn. For the lining use jap silk, which is a little expensive for the purpose, or a cheap, thin taffeta. Cut the garment in the fabric and the lining and place the lining pieces over the wrong side of the woollen fabric and baste tack together all over (see diagram). Then make the garment up as if it were a single layer of material only.

Lining

2) Use sewing silk thread for stitching woollen materials as the elasticity in the silk matches the stretch in the wool and will prevent seam stitching from breaking under the normal strains of wear.

3) Always press on the wrong side under a damp cloth. Any shininess which may occur on the right side may be removed with steam, using a damp cloth and a warm iron but NO pressure. Only a warm iron should be used at any time as steam, heat and pressure cause wool to felt up. Never press over pins, fastenings or tackings because impressions may be left which will be very difficult to remove.

4) Plain seams in very fine fabrics, e.g. Viyella, may be neatened with edge-stitching but be careful, when pressing, to leave no impression on the right side. After pressing the seam flat lift up each side and press again underneath it. On the whole, plain seams in woollen fabrics are best overcast. Jersey seams should be blanket stitched to prevent rolling. The seams of loosely-woven fabrics which fray badly must be bound with thin crossway strips of lawn or silk.

5) Hems in woollen fabrics show less if they are put up with skirt or crossway binding.

## MAN-MADE FIBRES

*Acetate, viscose and acrylics*

These yarns are used to produce an enormous variety of fabrics which can resemble cotton, linen, silk or wool. For each type of fabric the sewing instructions for the fibre it most closely resembles should be followed.

Some viscose and acetate frays very badly and should be cut out with pinking shears allowing extra large turnings. Those which resemble linen and lightweight woollens can be particularly trying to handle and all plain seams should be neatened with crossway binding for lasting results, if the fraying is very bad. Otherwise cut wider turnings than normal and neaten them temporarily on a zig-zag machine, so that they do not fray during handling. Later they can be trimmed and neatened finally with a machine overcast stitch.

### Pressing

A word of warning here. Always use a cool iron, at rayon setting. Iron on the wrong side as a permanent and unwanted shine can be produced. Excessive heat will damage the fibres — especially acetate. NEVER use a damping cloth for acetate and tricel as absolutely ineradicable watermarks may form. If a damping cloth is needed for any of the other fibres test it out thoroughly on a spare piece of material to make quite sure it is safe before using it on a garment.

*Polyamide and Polyester*

No preparation is required before cutting out as the fabrics are crease-resistant and should not even need pressing. Never attempt to tear the materials to get a straight end because the fibre is far too strong.

### Cutting Out

1) Whenever possible place pattern pieces so that the seams may be cut on the cross as they are then less likely to pucker when they are stitched.
2) Always allow extra wide turnings — not less than 2 cm as the materials fray easily.
3) For cutting use very sharp scissors or pinking shears. There is on the market, nowadays, a special tool for cutting these fabrics. It resembles an electric soldering-iron except that it has a small cutting blade at the end. After ten minutes heating the knife is hot enough to cut the fabric by melting the fibres without scorching them. The melted fibres fuse and seal the edge of the fabric so that it cannot fray. The sealing will withstand washing and therefore requires no further neatening. For transparent materials where any neatening would

show through, this is a great advantage. It is also a boon when working button-holes. The only disadvantage is that each pattern piece has to be cut out separately for if two thicknesses of fabric were cut together they would fuse together and become inseparable. Some protective covering, such as cardboard, must be placed under the fabric to protect the table from damage. When a synthetic fibre is mixed or blended with another fibre such as wool the tool cannot be used because it will not cut through the natural fibre which reacts differently to heat.

### Making Up

1) For a delicate fabric the fitting line is best traced out with flat tacking. In mixture fabrics tailor tacks can be used.

2) Use the finest possible machine and hand needles. The yarns are so fine that only the slimmest needles can penetrate between the threads without catching or pulling them.

3) Always use nylon or polyester sewing thread because other sewing threads are too thick and will not last the life of the fabric.

4) French seams or the run and fell types are the strongest and most satisfactory for these fabrics. Where a plain seam is used it should be finely overcast or edge-stitched, unless the fabric has been cut with the sealing tool.

5) Loosen both the upper and lower tensions on the sewing machine to produce a good stitch without puckering. Feed the material through the machine slowly without any forcing or it will pucker.

6) Always use trimmings, such as lace, bindings, elastic, ribbon, etc., which are made from the same fibres, otherwise tragedy may occur during laundering. For instance, if cotton lace is used to trim a nylon petticoat the heat required to iron the lace will melt the nylon. Also the lace will take longer to dry and will look coarse on such a dainty fabric.

7) When pressing be careful not to iron in unwanted creases as these can be removed only with a hotter iron which might damage the fabric. Use a damp cloth and a cool iron for pressing. If the cloth is not used the fabric may acquire a shininess which will be permanent.

### NET AND LACE

As lace can be made from cotton, wool, rayon, nylon or polyester yarns and net from the same yarns with the exception of wool, it is important to find out, when buying them, from which fibre they are made, so that the correct sewing thread can be used. Nylon and polyester threads are very strong and will cut through the threads of other fibres.

When these open mesh fabrics are made up with no backing the seams have to be as inconspicuous as possible because they will show through on the right side. Plain seams can be used and will show less if they are not neatened. Fortunately neither material frays so neatening is unnecessary. When piece lace or net and lace trimmings have to be pieced together as inconspicuously as possible it can be done as follows:

*Net.* On the wrong side, join up the two pieces of net with fine running stitches. Trim the turnings to 1-2 mm and whip over them closely.

*Lace.* With the right side uppermost, lap one piece over the other, matching the pattern. Tack carefully and then, with matching thread, oversew closely round the edges of the pattern through both layers of material. On the underside oversew again, crossing the previous stitches. Trim the turnings down to the stitching. This kind of join can be over-sewn by machine, using a swing needle machine or an attachment on an ordinary one.

When using a machine to stitch net and lace the tension must be loosened to avoid puckering and it is advisable to tack tissue paper behind the fabric before stitching to prevent the open mesh catching on the toothed machine feed and also to keep it from puckering. The paper can be torn away after stitching.

Lace is not a strong fabric and is more serviceable if backed with another fabric or with net. When dresses are made from all over lace, it is better to line them, instead of having a separate underslip. When this is done, the pattern pieces are cut out in both fabrics. The lace pieces are placed on top of the lining fabrics and both are baste tacked together all over, and, from then on, they are treated and made up as one single fabric. One of the advantages of this method is that the seams do not show through the lace. If lace is used for the brassiere tops of slips, it should be lined with net to give it a longer life. When slips are made entirely from nylon or polyester all over lace they are best lined with nylon or polyester tricot.

For net and lace curtains there is an elastic Ruffelette tape which will gather the top hems. This is very useful as when the fabric needs ironing after laundering the top hem can be stretched out and ironed flat. For polyester net a similar tape is made in polyester. A narrow hem must be made down each side of net curtains if the fabric is to keep its shape after washing.

## FIBREGLASS

1) Always sew all parts by machine. Loosen the tension and use a fairly long stitch (2-3 per cm). It may be necessary to tack tissue paper behind the finer fabrics before stitching. This can be torn away afterwards.

2) The manufacturers do not recommend the use of polyester or nylon sewing thread. This thread is stronger than the fabric and might damage it. Instead, use mercerized sewing cotton, size 60 or 70.

3) When curtains are lined with fabric other than fibreglass, it must be so attached that it can be removed and laundered separately.

4) Do not press hems heavily as this may crack and split the fibre.

## TRANSPARENT FABRICS

Here, again, the seams will show through on the right side so they must be very neat and as small as possible. French and run and fell seams are the most suitable and can be used for blouses and lingerie. When a plain seam must be used, very fine, regular overcasting will be the least noticeable finish. For underwear the pieces of fabric can be stitched together on the wrong side and the turnings trimmed to 1½ cm and neatened by using the satin stitch disc on a swing needle machine. This makes a very neat seam. Darts in transparent and sheer fabrics can also be finished in this way. A decorative type of seam for lingerie can be made with pin stitch. The turning is folded under on the fitting line on one piece of material and is laid over the turning of the other piece, right sides uppermost and the fitting lines matching. The two layers are tacked together and pin stitch is worked on the top. On the underside the turnings are cut away to the stitching.

The edges of these materials sometimes present difficulties, occasionally a hem looks heavy and clumsy, and then the edge can be rolled and whipped over. This is often done on the edges of handkerchiefs and chiffon scarves. Crisp materials, such as organdie, can have edges embroidered with scallops. Of course, lace and net edging can always be applied by various methods and embroidered edgings can be worked with swing needle machines.

Georgettes and chiffons are tricky fabrics to handle and the seams are more easily stitched if they are tacked to tissue paper, which can be torn away afterwards. A loose tension and very fine machine needles are essential for good results. The fabric threads are so fine that a needle which is too thick will hit the threads instead of passing between them and cause the fabric to pucker.

Pins are inclined to leave holes in these materials and it is wiser to use needles to hold seams together for tacking. The finest tacking cotton or silk thread should be used to tack parts up and small tacking stitches are best to hold the fabric together firmly.

When buttonholes are required they must be either worked ones or worked loops because the turnings of bound or piped buttonholes would show through. Buttons, snap fasteners or hooks can be used, but avoid zip fasteners because the tape is too heavy.

## PILE FABRICS

### Velvets, Velveteens, Needlecord, Corduroy

These fabrics have a raised pile which runs in one direction only, downwards for velveteen, needlecord and corduroy and upwards for chiffon velvet. This means that pattern pieces cannot be placed upside down to fit in with each other for economical cutting, and therefore extra material must be purchased to allow for this and there will be a certain amount of waste.

Pins may leave marks in the fabrics, so parts should be held together with needles. Also, for the same reason, it is best to tack with sewing silk. The tacking must be firm (a short and a longer stitch alternately) because the pile causes the top layer to 'walk' along the under one. When machining, keep the needles holding the pieces of fabric together, placed at intervals across the tacking and take the machine needle over them very carefully as they are encountered. This helps to prevent the presser foot pushing the top layer along.

Pressing seams can be a problem if no velvet board is available. Velveteen, needlecord and corduroy are not so difficult because they can be pressed very lightly on the wrong side under a damp cloth. On no account must this treatment be given to silk velvets because the pile will be flattened and iron marks may be left. Get a second person to hold one end of the seam while you hold the other and then pass an iron, preferably a steam iron, over the seam on the wrong side.

Plain seams are best for these fabrics, although overlaid seams can be used on needlecord and corduroy, but, as a rule outside stitching disturbs and flattens the pile. Plain seams can be neatened by overcasting them or by binding them with thin crossway silk material.

Hems in these fabrics can be put up with crossway or Paris binding. In the heavier corduroys the hem is best put up flat and fixed in place with herringbone stitch.

# FUR FABRICS

There are many fabrics made from wool or man-made fibres which imitate fur and the following points should be remembered when making them up.

1) The pile or fur part is fixed into a woven or knitted base and, if the pile is deep and the material is cut in the normal way, the fur may be clipped short at the edges. To prevent this, pin the pattern pieces on to the wrong side and cut round them through one thickness of fabric only with an extremely sharp penknife, just cutting through the base fabric and then the fur pile will pull apart intact.

2) When parts are tacked together for stitching, the tacking must be small and firm otherwise the pile will cause the top layer of fabric to move along on the under layer.

3) Use a fairly large machine stitch, about two stitches to the centimetre and test the tension before stitching up.

4) To make the seams as invisible as possible the pile should be combed over them on the right side.

# JERSEY FABRICS

Knitted fabrics can be made from most types of yarn. They behave rather differently from woven fabrics, having much more stretch in both directions and this makes cutting out less easy and may cause seams to drop and stretch out of shape in wear.

## Preparation Before Cutting Out

Wool jerseys should be damp pressed to shrink them, but jerseys made from synthetic fibres do not need this treatment because they do not shrink at all and damp heat may damage the fibres.

## Cutting Out

Lay the fabric out flat and let it be completely relaxed, for if it is stretched at this stage the garment may become too small when it is made up. Wool jerseys are often knitted in a tubular shape and this can make cutting out more economical because pattern pieces can be placed to any where on the fabric by just turning it round. All knitted fabrics should be cut cleanly with very sharp scissors.

## Making Up

1) Knitted dress fabrics are often better lined throughout. Synthetic fabrics should be lined with materials made from synthetic yarns so that they may react in the same way to sewing and laundry processes. For interlinings the non-woven types are very suitable.

2) When dress fabrics are unlined the seams should be taped to prevent them stretching and sagging. The taping should be carried out with crossway strips, 1 cm wide, cut from some thin material or with purchased bias binding cut in half lengthwise. It is wiser to use crossway strips instead of straight ones so that the seams may be a little elastic. Strips cut on the straight would tighten the seams up too much. Place the strip centrally over the fitting line on the wrong side of the fabric and tack and stitch it in with the seam, see diagram.

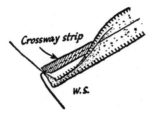

3) Use fine machine needles, size 14, and sew wool, silk and rayon jerseys with pure sewing silk, cotton with mercerized cotton thread and synthetic fibres with nylon or polyester sewing threads.

4) Jersey fabrics do not fray but the seams are neater if they are finished off, as they tend to roll under. Blanket stitch the seams of dress weight jerseys or better still, overcast them by machine. Lingerie fabrics, particularly the transparent ones such as nylon tricot should have the smallest possible seams. These are best stitched as for a plain seam with the turnings trimmed to 3-6 mm. These can be neatened together with very fine close blanket stitch or with machine overcasting.

5) Tack garments up and fit them very carefully before stitching so that they will not have to be unpicked and altered. Unpicking seams in jersey fabrics is a difficult business and the material is liable to become cut.

6) Sometimes hems are a problem because it is not easy to avoid the stitches showing on the right side. When they are turned up and finished with crossway or skirt binding the slip hemming should be loose enough to 'give' with the stretch in the fabric. The least visible method is as follows:

*a)* Neaten the raw hem edge with blanket stitch or with machine overcasting.

*b)* Tack the hem in position ½ cm below the neatened edge.

*c)* Turn back the top hem edge as far as the tacking and take small stitches alternately in the hem and the garment. Do not pull the stitching too tight. Then let the hem edge fall back against the garment, see diagram.

W.S.

## FABRICS WITH CHECK AND STRIPE PATTERNS

If the checks and stripes are not symmetrical the pattern pieces will have to be placed in one direction only and extra material will be needed. If the checks are very large, more material will again be required to match them up.

Where checks and stripes meet at seams they must be matched exactly and the easiest way to ensure this is as follows:

1) Pin the seam together by placing the pins across the seam at intervals matching the check or stripe on both pieces of fabric exactly.

2) Tack carefully checking constantly to make sure the pattern matches everywhere. Keep the pins in.

3) Machine the seam taking the needle carefully over each pin as it is met. The pins will stop the presser-foot pushing the top layer of fabric along and disarranging the stripes and checks.

## FABRICS WHICH FRAY BADLY (HEAVY LINENS, VISCOSE LINENS, ETC.)

Heavy art and dress linens, viscose linens, some wool-like viscose and nylon all fray very quickly and this can be partly checked if cutting out is done with pinking shears, allowing slightly wider turnings than the pattern gives. After stitching, when seams are ready to be neatened the pinking can be trimmed off. When articles will be handled a great deal, as in embroidery, a temporary hem can be tacked in.

Plain seams are best neatened with crossway binding as overcasting may pull further threads away.

Before making buttonholes, interline the fabric with an iron-on type of stiffening which will hold the threads and stop them fraying. The buttonhole is then much more easily worked.

## STITCHING STRETCH FABRICS

Sew these fabrics with polyester sewing thread as they require a strong thread which will 'give' with the stretch. Lower the tension of the machine stitch as much as possible consistent with getting a good stitch.

When stitching in the direction of the stretch pull the fabric taut. This will produce a slightly looser stitch which will not split in wear when the material is fully extended.

Modern sewing machines usually have special machine stitches for sewing these fabrics. If the machine does not have a stretch stitch but will zig-zag, use a very slight zig-zag setting for stitching seams and this will have a little 'give'.

## PLASTIC SHEETING AND PLASTIC COATED FABRICS

1) Pins must not be used as they leave permanent marks.
2) Keep pattern pieces in place for cutting out with weights.
3) Pieces cannot be tacked together because the needle will leave holes. Instead use the slip-on type of paper clip or Sellotape.
4) Use a long machine stitch, not more than eight per inch because, if the plastic is not backed with fabric, it will tear like perforated paper.
5) Plastic has a slightly sticky surface and it should be sprinkled with French chalk or talcum powder to ease its way through the machine.
6) Place tissue paper underneath the plastic when machining to prevent the toothed edge of the feed dog marking it.
7) Whenever possible finish the edges of unbacked plastic with cotton crossway binding to give extra strength.
8) Never press it as the heat of the iron will melt it.

### Plastic-Coated Cotton

This fabric presents a few problems:
1) The plastic side of the fabric sticks to the machine and does not feed through freely so that when outside stitching is necessary, the machine plate and needle should be oiled with machine oil. As the fabric is waterproof the oil will not harm it although the sewing cotton may become a trifle oily. Be careful to wipe the machine thoroughly afterwards.

If the machine has a roller foot attachment or a foot coated with Teflon this problem of sticking does not arise and oiling is not necessary.
2) Stitched and turned-out edges do not press flat but tend to roll. They should therefore be flattened with outside edge stitching.
3) The fabric presses easily on the wrong side under a cloth but keep the temperature of the iron low, otherwise the plastic coating may melt.
4) Be careful not to stretch printed fabrics as the pattern loses some of its colour density and never recovers.
5) Avoid too many seams — keep styles simple.

# 8 Washing and Cleaning Fabrics

The principal agents used for washing and cleaning fabrics are as follows:

## SOAP

Soap is an alkaline substance which helps water to wet and penetrate more readily and, therefore, to clean it more thoroughly. The dirt comes out of the fabric and the soap absorbs it. If hard water is used, soluble salts in the water prevent the soap lathering properly and lessen its cleaning power and a scum is formed which can discolour the fabric. In districts where the water is hard, it should be softened with soda, ammonia, borax or a specially prepared softener such as Calgon, when soap is used. Soap lathers and cleans best in warm or hot water.

## SOAP POWDERS

Most of these contain bleaching agents and, very often, soda. Therefore they must be used with discrimination, especially for fabrics which can be harmed by bleaches and soda.

## SOAPLESS DETERGENTS

These are quite different from soaps as they are made from chemicals and are not alkaline. They clean equally well in hard or soft water which may be cold, warm or hot. They are very useful for cleaning fabrics such as wool and rayons, which are harmed by alkalies and hot water.

## ALKALIES

*Washing soda,* used to soften hard water and to remove grease and scorch stains.
*Borax.* A very mild agent used to soften hard water, to remove stains, such as tea stains, and to give a slight stiffness to some fabrics.
*Ammonia.* Used for softening water and to remove grease and vegetable stains.
*Bicarbonate of soda.* Another very mild alkali used to soften water and to neutralize acids.

## ACIDS

*Oxalic acid and salts of lemon.* Highly poisonous powders which are used to remove iron mould and obstinate stains.

*Vinegar.* This is a form of acetic acid used to revive colours, to stiffen silks and to neutralize alkalies.

## BLEACHES

Bleaches are divided into two main groups:
1) Oxidizing bleaches which whiten fabrics by releasing and adding oxygen which makes colour and discoloration disappear.
2) Reducing bleaches which remove colour by taking oxygen away from it. However, if the fabric is hung up to dry out of doors, it can take up oxygen from the air and the stain or colour may reappear.

### Oxidizing Bleaches

*a) Sunlight.* The natural way to bleach fabric is to hang it up out of doors or to lay it on the grass. Then the oxygen in the air combines with the sunlight and moisture in the fabric to make it white. This bleaching action can also cause coloured articles to fade.

*b) Hydrogen peroxide.* This is a mild bleach which is very useful because it can be used on silk and wool fabrics without causing damage. It can be bought in 10-volume strength and must be stored in a coloured bottle in a dark place, otherwise it will lose its strength. Before it can be used safely it should be diluted with ten times as much water.

*c) Potassium permanganate.* Another bleach useful for removing mildew and perspiration from silk and wool as well as from other fibres. It is a purple crystal and for use on silk and wool, dissolve 1 g in ½ litre of warm water, and for cotton and linen, dissolve 2 g in ½ litre of hot water. If the solution is poured on to the stain it liberates oxygen to bleach it out and leaves behind a brown stain, which, in its turn, has to be removed with another bleach. This can be done with oxalic acid or with a solution made up of 1 part of 10-volume hydrogen peroxide, 4 parts of water and 1 teaspoon of vinegar. It must be rinsed out well afterwards.

*d) Sodium hypochlorite.* This is a bleaching solution made from chloride of lime (bleaching powder), soda and water. It is a strong chlorine bleach which liberates a lot of oxygen and must not be used in a concentrated solution or the fabrics will become tender. It is suitable for use on cotton, linen and cellulose rayon only. Chlorine bleaches must never be used on silk, wool or nylon.

*e) Sodium perborate.* This is the bleach which is added to synthetic detergents and soap powders to give extra brightness to white articles. It can be used on most fabrics.

### Reducing Bleaches

*Sodium hyposulphite.* A strong bleaching agent which may be used safely on most fibres. It takes up oxygen from the air and turns it into sodium meta-bisulphite, which splits up into sodium sulphate and sulphur dioxide and takes the colour out of stains by withdrawing oxygen.

*Note:* When alkalies have been used on fabrics (e.g. silk or wool) which they might damage, should they be allowed to dry in and become concentrated, they should be neutralized with acid. To do this, rinse in 5 litres of water to which a tablespoon of vinegar (acetic acid) has been added.

When acid has been used on cotton or linen the fibres may become tender unless the acid is neutralized with an alkali. For instance, after using salts of lemon to remove a stain, bicarbonate of soda should be rubbed over the spot to neutralize the acid.

When bleaches have been used they must be rinsed out thoroughly — boiled out if possible — to remove every trace.

| Cleaning Agent | Fabrics on which it should not be used |
|---|---|
| Acetic acid. | Acetate as it will dissolve the fibre. |
| Acetone. | Acetate as it will dissolve the fibre. |
| Ammonia. | Test on viscose and acetate before using. |
| Boiling water. | Silk, wool and some man-made fibres. |
| Borax. | Viscose and acetate |
| Hydrogen peroxide. | Nylon. |
| Methylated spirits. | Test on man-made fibres before using. |
| Soda. | Silk, wool. |
| Sodium hypochlorite. | Silk, wool, nylon. |
| Vinegar. | May dull the lustre of viscose and acetate. |
| Trichlorethylene. | Triacetate. |
| Perchloroethylene | P.V.C. and P.V.C. coated fabrics. |

## CLEANING AGENTS SUITABLE FOR MOST FIBRES

*Benzine.* Used to remove grease.
*Carbon tetrachloride.* Also used for grease spots.
*Glycerine.* Used to loosen vegetable stains.
*Paraffin.* Removes paint.
*Trichlorethylene.* Used to remove grease.
*Turpentine.* Removes paint stains.
*White spirit.* Cleans P.V.C. and coated fabrics.

## STAIN REMOVAL

Before any article is washed it should be looked over for stains which may not come out with ordinary washing and these should be dealt with first. As far as possible all stains should be treated as soon as they occur because they are so much more easily removed when they are fresh. If they are allowed to penetrate and dry into the fabric more drastic measures may have to be taken to remove them which may harm the fibres. If uncertain about removing a stain take it to professional cleaners because stains can be further set in with inexpert treatment.

### Points to Consider when Removing Stains

1) What kind of stain is it?
2) What is the safest agent most likely to remove it? Always try the mildest ones first.
3) Of what yarn or yarns is the fabric made?
4) Has it any special finish or colour which the agent might remove?

With the many new fabrics which are being continually produced the removal of stains becomes more and more complicated. Not only are new fibres produced but several different fibres may be blended or mixed together in one fabric. For example, a fabric may be made up of wool, acetate and cotton fibres, all of which react differently to various cleaning agents. If acetone is used to remove a nail varnish stain from such a fabric, the acetate fibres will dissolve while the others remain unaffected — if soda is used to remove a grease spot, the wool will be damaged, the acetate may lose its lustre and the cotton will be unharmed. Therefore it is very important to know from which fibres a fabric is made so that stain removal agents safe for all the fibres may be used. Furthermore, certain agents, such as starch and bleaches, must not be used when fabrics have been treated with certain special finishes, e.g. flameproofing, crease-resist and so on, otherwise the finish may be damaged. When making up garments it is a good plan to tack in somewhere a small embroidered label which states the kind of yarn and any special finish, because in the course of time it is not always easy to remember all these details. Garments ready made from fabrics needing special washing care are usually so labelled.

The stains most commonly encountered are:

*a) Vegetable stains.* Fruit juice, grass, tea, coffee, cocoa, wine.
*b) Protein stains.* Blood, egg, milk.
*c) Greasy stains.* Hair oil, fat, lipstick.
*d) Paint stains.* Oil paint, cellulose paint, emulsion paint, nail varnish, tar.
*e) Miscellaneous.* Ink (writing, ball point, Indian and red), iron mould, scorch, perspiration, mildew.

### Vegetable Stains

*Fresh Stain*

Sprinkle salt over the damp stain to stop it spreading.

*White cotton and linen.*
1) Stretch over a basin, spread with salt and pour boiling water through.
2) Wash and rinse.
*Coloured cotton and linen, white and coloured wool and silk*
1) Spread with glycerine.
2) Steep in warm water with 1 teaspoon of borax dissolved in each ½ litre.
3) Wash and rinse.
*Man-made fibres*
1) Apply glycerine and leave for a while.
2) Dab with vinegar (Not on acetate).
3) Wash and rinse.

*Dried-In Stains*

*White cotton and linen*
1) Stretch the stain over a basin, damp it and very gently, with a PLASTIC spoon (not a metal one) rub in either oxalic acid or salts of lemon crystals.
2) Pour boiling water through.
3) Neutralize the acid by rubbing in bicarbonate of soda or by pouring over a weak ammonia solution.
4) Wash, boil and rinse.
*White silk and wool*
1) Sponge with diluted hydrogen of peroxide or use hyposulphite bleach.
2) Wash and rinse.
*White man-made fibres*
1) Sponge with oxalic acid solution (1 teaspoon in ½ litre of warm water).
2) Neutralize with ammonia if it is safe to use on the fabric.
3) Wash and rinse.

**Grass Stain**

Treat with methylated spirits and then wash.

**Protein Stains**

*Fresh Stain*

1) Steep in cold water and salt (Hot water coagulates the protein and sets it, making it more difficult to remove).
2) Wash the fabric. Linen and cotton can be boiled if necessary.
*Note.* If a paste of starch and water is spread over fresh bloodstains they will be absorbed.

*Obstinate Stains*

Steep in hyposulphite bleach (1 teaspoon in ½ litre of warm or hot water according to the fabric).

## Greasy Stains

If grease has congealed into a solid lump scrape it off with the back of a knife.
*Cotton and linen*
Steep in hot water and synthetic detergent to emulsify the grease. Wash or boil.
*Wool, silk and man-made fibres.*
Wash with warm water and synthetic detergent.
*Unwashable fabrics*
1) Place the stain over clean blotting paper and press with a warm iron which will melt the grease and drive it through to be absorbed by the blotting paper which must be moved from time to time. Repeat until all the grease has disappeared.
2) Place over blotting paper and apply carbon tetrachloride or trichlorethylene on a pad. Rub gently from the outside towards the centre until the stain has been driven through to the blotting paper.
3) Proceed as for 2 but use synthetic detergent dissolved in warm water on a cloth. Rinse afterwards with clean water on a cloth.

## Paint Stains

*Oil paint*

1) Place the stain over blotting paper and sponge with turpentine or paraffin on a rag.
2) Wash with synthetic detergent and rinse.

*Cellulose paint and nail varnish*

Sponge with acetone. Wash and rinse. Acetone cannot be used on acetate fabric but amyl acetate may be used.

*Emulsion paint*

1) When it is fresh, soak in cold water and wash.
2) When it has dried in, steep in methylated spirits and then wash.

*Tar*

1) Place the stain over clean blotting paper.
2) Sponge with carbon tetrachloride.

3) If the stain has dried in, rub with lard to soften it before using the cleaning agent.

### Miscellaneous Stains

*Writing ink*

*Cotton and linen*
1) Spread with lemon juice and salt, leave for a time and then wash.
2) If the stain has really dried in, use oxalic acid or salts of lemon.
*Silk and wool*
1) Fresh stains can be steeped in milk or methylated spirits and then washed in warm water and synthetic detergent.
2) Obstinate stains may have to be bleached out with potassium permanganate and the resulting brown stain must be removed with hydrogen peroxide and vinegar, see page 115. Wash and rinse well.
3) Hyposulphite bleach could be used.
*Man-made fibres*
Steep in milk and wash with synthetic detergent.

*Red ink*
Steep in ammonia, borax, oxalic acid solution or in hyposulphite bleach.

*Indian ink*

Sometimes, if the stains are fresh, they will wash out. Obstinate stains may be loosened by steeping in turpentine and finally cleaned with carbon tetrachloride. If these treatments fail, have the garment professionally cleaned.

*Ball-Point ink*

Sponge with methylated spirits, benzene, carbon tetrachloride or trichlorethylene, and then wash in water and synthetic detergent.

*Iron mould*

Remove with salts of lemon, oxalic acid or hyposulphite bleach, according to the fabric.

*Scorch*

*Linen and cotton.* Steep in soda and hot water or in hypochlorite bleach. Wash thoroughly or boil.

*Silk, wool and man-made fibres.* Sponge with diluted hydrogen peroxide or hyposulphite bleach.

*Perspiration and mildew*

Use potassium permanganate and bleach the brown stain out with hydrogen peroxide, see page 115.

## WASHING COTTON AND LINEN FABRICS

Cottons and linens are amongst the easiest materials to wash because they are not harmed by the usual cleaning agents and the fibres become stronger when they are wet and are, therefore, able to stand up to the friction of rubbing and even of scrubbing when it is necessary to remove very dirty stains.

### Steeping

Household cottons and linens which are white and those in which the colours are fast can be steeped in cold water for a few hours before washing as this will loosen the dirt so that it can be easily washed out. Cold water is the best for this purpose and it is able to penetrate the fabric and loosen the dirt more thoroughly if a little synthetic detergent is added to it. The detergent must be completely dissolved before the clothes are put into the water because dry detergent powder is concentrated and may harm the fibres. It does not matter whether the water is hard or soft for steeping.

### Hard Water

If synthetic detergent is used for washing the fabrics, hard water will clean as effectively as soft water, but when soap is used the water must be softened because hard water and soap form an insoluble scum which may penetrate the fabrics and make them a dirty grey colour.

### Heat

Linens and cottons are unaffected by high temperatures, short of scorching, therefore they can be washed in very hot water and can be boiled to improve the colour and to sterilize them. Before boiling, dirty marks, which have been loosened by steeping, can be scrubbed with a brush on a rubbing-board to remove them.

## Acids

Properly used acids cause no damage but they must be well rinsed out of the material afterwards, for if they are left to dry in it, they will become concentrated and may damage the fibres.

## Alkalies

These are harmless unless they are used too often in too big doses when they may discolour the fabrics. For instance, when soda is used to soften hard water, only just the right amount necessary should be used. The amount will depend on the degree of hardness of the water and this can be found out from the local water authority.

## Bleaches

Most bleaches may be used safely provided they are well rinsed out afterwards otherwise they will concentrate in the fabric and may rot the fibres.

## Starching

Most household articles such as tablecloths, dinner napkins, etc., are the better for starching, both linen and cotton. Ginghams and some other lightweight summer dress materials also benefit with starching but make sure that the fabric has not been given one of the special finishes which should not be starched. Some of the permanently glazed and flameproofed fabrics must not be starched and neither must those which have been permanently stiffened, such as organdie.

## Washing Machines

Most linens and cottons, except those with a velvet pile, can be washed in washing machines and can be dried in spin-driers. In fact spin-driers produce the even dampness which is ideal for ironing.

## Ironing

Both linens and cotton require a hot iron for the best results. If a sheen is required linens should be ironed on the right side while damp. If the fabric becomes too dry for ironing, it should be damped down all over and rolled up for a time to spread the dampness evenly. A steam iron is a great help when the fabric has become a little dry. Never iron folds in linen fabrics because the fibres are inclined to crack and split and it is usually along the folds that tablecloths and napkins show the first signs of wear. This happens because there is no elasticity in linen fibres.

*Coloured and printed cottons and linens*

These should be washed a little more carefully than white fabrics bearing in mind the following points:

1) Do not steep when colours are likely to run, and wash as quickly as possible.

2) Acids and alkalies may affect colours so use with due care.

3) Heat fades colours and friction loosens them. Wash more gently in cooler water.

4) Do not use bleaches and be careful when removing stains. Try out stain removal agents on a part which will not show before using on noticeable parts.

*Velveteen, corduroy, needlecord*

These fabrics require rather different treatment from other cotton fabrics. Wash by moving up and down in soapy or detergent water so that the water passes through the fabric and loosens the dirt. Do not squeeze, wring or rub. Rinse first in warm water to remove the soap and then in cold water to improve the colour without wringing or rubbing. Hang up dripping wet to dry. Spin-driers should not be used for these materials because they produce a creased effect which is difficult to iron out. Corduroy and needlecord can be ironed normally on the wrong side and velveteen is best ironed over a velvet board.

*Seersucker and plissé*

These materials can be washed normally but they should not require ironing as this might flatten the puckered stripes or pattern.

All the foregoing rules about washing cotton and linen apply to fabrics which have not been specially treated with crease- or shrink-resist, etc., finishes. Where fabrics have been so treated, the washing instructions which are usually supplied with them, must be followed carefully, otherwise the finish may be spoiled. For washing instructions for various finishes see pages 134 - 135.

## WASHING SILK FABRICS

Silks are lovely fabrics and usually expensive. Therefore they should be very carefully washed to make them last as long as possible. Stiff taffetas, organza, velvet and fabrics where the colours run should always be dry-cleaned because, besides causing colours to run, washing destroys stiffness and will ruin the pile of velvet.

### Steeping

Prolonged and repeated steeping may turn white silks yellowish, therefore they should be steeped for not longer than fifteen minutes in lukewarm water and synthetic detergent. Do not use soap for steeping because it is alkaline and may harm the fibres.

### Hard Water

Silks are best washed with synthetic detergents as they are not alkaline, in which case hard water does no harm. However if soap is used the water must be softened to prevent the silk becoming discoloured and borax, which is only a mild alkali, is the best softener — never use soda which is too strong and harmful.

### Heat

Excessive heat is harmful because it will turn white silk yellow. Never boil silk, use only lukewarm water, dry away from direct heat and use a moderate iron.

### Acids

Concentrated acids can destroy the fibres but dilute acids are not harmful, though they are absorbed and retained by the fibres, particularly in the case of wild silks. Acetic acid — 1 tablespoon of vinegar in 5 litres of water — used as the final rinse will restore the scroop of silk after it has been washed.

### Alkalies

These discolour the silk and make it tender. Hot caustic soda will dissolve the fibre completely. However, ammonia can be used with safety.

### Bleaches

The natural yellow colour of silk is very hard to bleach and a pure white silk is not easy to obtain. Only mild bleaches, such as hydrogen peroxide, can be used. Chlorine should never be used as it destroys the fibre.

### General Washing Rules

1) Always wash silk before it becomes badly soiled.
2) Steep for fifteen minutes in lukewarm synthetic detergent solution.
3) Wash in lukewarm water with synthetic detergent, very gently — do not rub, wring or twist — just squeeze the water through the garment. If a washing machine is used the silk must be tied up loosely in a muslin bag.
4) Rinse first in warm water without wringing. If soap has been used the water must be soft and the rinsing thorough because alkali drying in the fabric will become concentrated and rot it.
5) Rinse finally in cold water as this brings the spring back into silk and 1 tablespoon of vinegar to every 5 litres restores the scroop.
6) Some unweighted, cultivated silks are very light and may need stiffening

after washing. This can be done by giving a final rinse in warm water in which stationer's gum has been dissolved in the proportion of 1-4 teaspoons of gum to every ½ litre of water, according to the degree of stiffness required.
7) To dry, roll the silk up in a towel or cloth which will absorb the surplus moisture. After this treatment thin silks can usually be ironed straight away but heavier fabrics will have to be hung up to dry a little more.

## Ironing

Use a warm iron and wherever possible iron on the wrong side to avoid getting an unwanted shine on the right side. Never iron over seams or double parts — use sleeve and skirt boards — otherwise shiny impressions may be made. Always have cultivated silks evenly damp all over because if some parts are more damp than others, watermarks will be ironed in. For this reason silk should never be damped down. (When making up silk fabrics do not use a damp pressing cloth). Wild silks — antung, shantung, tussore — should be ironed when quite dry because they watermark very easily and if ironed wet acquire a papery texture. If a good finish cannot be obtained when they are dry, try using a steam iron, but test it out on a spare piece of fabric first.

Do not iron in unnecessary creases as this may cause the fibres to crack and split.
*Georgette and crêpe silks* contract and lose their shape when washed and must be ironed back into shape with great care.
*Printed silks.* Before attempting to wash printed silks test for colour fastness. Damp a small part, such as the inside of the hem. Place a white cloth over the damp patch and iron it dry with a warm iron. If any colour from the pattern comes off on to the white cloth do not wash the silk but have it dry cleaned.
*Moiré silk.* The watered pattern is printed on with rollers and will disappear at the first washing, therefore it should be dry-cleaned.

## WASHING WOOLLEN MATERIALS

Woollens require more careful washing than most other fabrics. Only those fabrics such as serge, nun's veiling, flannel, some knitted fabrics and mixtures like Viyella, worsted and polyester, etc., wash satisfactorily. Tweeds and heavy woollens are best dry-cleaned. The important points to remember when washing wool are:
1) It is inclined to shrink.
2) When twisted and rubbed in the presence of heat and moisture the overlapping scales of the fibres become inseparably interlocked with each other causing the fabric to thicken, felt up and become dense.

### Steeping

As long exposure to water causes shrinking, woollens should only be steeped if they are very dirty and then for not longer than fifteen minutes in lukewarm water containing synthetic detergent. Do not use soapy water for steeping because it is alkaline and harmful.

### Hard Water

Hard water is inclined to make wool harsh and should be softened by using either 2 teaspoons of ammonia or 4 teaspoons of borax to 5 litres. Wool is washed best with synthetic detergent because this is more easily rinsed out than soap and leaves the fabric so very much softer.

### Heat

To avoid felting use only warm water, 32°C. Do not dry in front of direct heat because 'yellowing' may occur. Use only a warm iron.

### Acids

Dilute acids are absorbed into the fibres but are not harmful, beyond making soap more difficult to rinse out.

### Alkalies

Alkalies such as soda make wool harsh and discolour it. Hot caustic soda will dissolve the fibres. Mild alkalies like ammonia and borax can be used safely for softening water if used in the right quantities.

### Bleaches

Only mild bleaches, e.g. hydrogen of peroxide, should be used. Chlorine is harmful and makes the fabric yellow instead of white.

### General Washing Rules

1) Steep only when necessary for not more than fifteen minutes.
2) Wash in warm water and synthetic detergent, very gently by squeezing the water through the fabric. DO NOT rub, twist or wring in any way and do not hold a garment up when it is heavy with water because the weight will elongate it and pull it out of shape. Keep under the water all the time.
3) Rinse as many times as is necessary to remove every trace of detergent.

*Note.* Woollen fabrics may be washed in a washing machine but the temperature of the water must be carefully controlled.

4) Spin-drying is excellent for removing all surplus moisture and therefore reducing the weight so that the fabric can be hung up to finish drying without fear of its being pulled out of shape. Alternatively it can be put through a wringer, but NEVER wring out or twist by hand. During drying shake the fabric from time to time to fluff out the hairy fibres. When knitted woollens stretch very much they must be dried flat.

### Ironing

Iron on the wrong side while slightly damp, with a warm iron. Try to avoid ironing over seams or double thicknesses because shiny impressions may be left. If the fabric becomes too dry a steam iron is very helpful.

Air thoroughly — for twenty-four hours — because wool holds moisture imperceptibly.

### Durably Pleated Wool

Do not use a washing machine, wringer or spin-dryer. Hang up wet to drip dry. Do not iron.

### Wool Mixed or Blended with Other Fibres

Wash as for pure wool, which will be the more delicate fibre.

### Superwash Wool

Wash in a washing machine in warm water 40°C. Spin as dry as possible but DO NOT wring by hand. Use a warm iron only.

## WASHING VISCOSE AND CUPRO

Viscose and Cupro are affected by chemicals in much the same way as cotton fabrics. Wash in warm water, 40°C, and use a medium-hot iron, setting 180°C.

The main point to remember is that viscose and acetate fibres are weak when they are wet. This means that they must not be rubbed, wrung or twisted in any way and must receive only the gentlest treatment when wet and the weight must be supported all the time.

### Hard Water

If soap is used, soften hard water with borax or ammonia because soda spoils the lustre of silky fabrics.

### Heat

Most viscose should be washed in hot water 60°C but for knitted and light-weight fabrics which may be more sensitive to heat, use hand-hot water 48°C.

### Acids

These can be safely used, including salts of lemon provided they are rinsed out thoroughly afterwards.

### Alkalies

Avoid the use of alkalies when possible because they spoil the lustre of silky fabrics. For this reason, synthetic detergents are better than soap for washing these materials. Hot caustic soda damages the fibres although it does not actually destroy them.

### Bleaches

Have no effect on the fibres.

### General Washing Rules

1) Wash as for silk. For the more delicate rayon fabrics it is unwise to use washing machines or spin-dryers on account of the weakness of the fibre when wet.
2) Wash gently by squeezing under the water and support the weight throughout.
3) Rinse well, still supporting the fabric.
4) Squeeze gently and remove surplus water by rolling in a towel or use a tumbler or spin-drier for a short time only. Hang up to dry, but not in the sun as sunlight rots the fibres.

### Ironing

Use a medium-hot iron, rayon setting, and iron on the wrong side as viscose fabrics can develop a high lustre on the side on which they are ironed. The fabric should be evenly damp to avoid watermarks being ironed in. Never damp down. If the fabric becomes too dry it is difficult to get a good finish though a steam iron will often help.

*Viscose knitted fabric*
Heavy jerseys seldom need ironing but lightweight materials should be ironed dry on the wrong side.

*Viscose crêpes* may shrink up when wet and will have to be ironed very carefully back into the original shape.
*Viscose velvets* should be dry-cleaned.

## WASHING ACETATE

Acetate must be washed with rather more care than viscose or cuprammonium as it reacts differently to heat and some chemicals. Acetone dissolves the fibres and should not be used for dry-cleaning. Be careful not to upset nail varnish remover (which is acetone) over acetate fabric.

### Heat

Too much heat can have a disastrous effect. Really hot water can damage the fibre and a hot iron can melt it. Therefore use warm water always, 40°C.

### Acids

Glacial acetic acid will dissolve the fibres. Do not use it for dry-cleaning.

### General Washing Rules

1) Wash gently in warm water.
2) Do not wring or twist as the fibre is weaker when wet.
3) Rinse well and absorb surplus moisture by rolling in a towel.
4) Iron when damp with a warm iron. It is most important that the dampness is even because otherwise permanent watermarks will appear. If the fabric becomes too dry never damp down but re-wet it again completely. Do not iron over fastenings as they will leave shiny impressions and may even cut through the fabric. Avoid ironing in unnecessary creases because they will be difficult to iron out.
5) Dirt and dust can damage the fibres therefore do not let the fabric become too soiled before washing.
6) When acetate is mixed or blended with another fibre wash as though it were 100 per cent acetate.

## WASHING TRICEL

Tricel is dirt resistant but like all man-made fibres it should be washed before it becomes really dirty; 100 per cent Tricel should be washed by hand as washing machines may make creases and the less the fabric is creased when it is wet the easier it will be to iron. Never use bleach.

1) Wash in 40°C warm water mild with detergent or soapflakes.

2) Do not wring or squeeze the fabric.

3) Rinse in warm water, dry in a tumbler drier, running it cold before switching it off. If using a spin-drier, rinse in COLD water first and spin for one minute only. Pleated Tricel should be drip-dried.

4) When ironing is necessary the fabric must be really damp. A steam iron gives a very good finish.

*Tricel + another fibre.* When a fabric is a mixture or blend containing tricel it can be machine washed and tumbler dried, provided it is not permanently pleated. Never use a spin-dryer nor put through a wringer.

*Tricel wadding.* This washes well without becoming lumpy or flat. It springs back into its original fluffy state.

*Dry-cleaning.* The fibre dry-cleans satisfactorily but always label it 'Tricel' so that the cleaner will know which chemicals to use.

## WASHING POLYAMIDE FABRICS

Nylon is a strong fibre — as strong when wet as it is when dry — and is easy to wash as it does not have to be handled especially gently.

### Heat

100 per cent nylon is not harmed by wet heat or steam but excessive heat, 225°C will melt the fibre. If nylon is boiled the fibres will not be damaged but creases which may form in the fabric during the boiling will become set with the heat and will be difficult to iron out because the heat required to remove them would destroy the fibre.

### Acids

Dilute acids can be used, e.g. salts of lemon, but concentrated acids cause loss of strength.

### Alkalies

Cold alkalies have no effect. Hot caustic soda is harmful.

### Bleaches

Never use bleaches — they damage the fibres.

### General Washing Rules

1) Wash often before the garments are too soiled otherwise the dirt which is picked up and held by the static electricity in the fabric may be difficult to

remove completely and will cause discoloration.

2) Wash coloured nylon in hand-hot water using detergent or soap, and white nylon separately in hot water. Never use bleach. Nylon should be washed separately from fabrics made from other fibres.

3) Rinse thoroughly. The moisture does not penetrate the fabric but runs off it. Surplus moisture can be absorbed by rolling in a towel. Spin-dryers should be used only just long enough to remove the surface moisture, because if drying is carried out for longer creases will form.

4) Hang up to dry away from direct heat which might cause discoloration and out of the sun which rots the fibres.

5) Nylon jersey, nylon tricot and woven crinkled nylon fabrics seldom require ironing unless they are very much creased up during the washing and drying. Plain fabrics look better if touched up. This should be done when the fabric is practically dry with a COOL iron. It is quite safe to damp down or to use a damping cloth because nylon does not watermark. Do not iron in unwanted creases as they can be removed only by a higher temperature which may damage the fabric. A steam iron is often helpful to remove creases.

*Nylon + another fibre.* Blended and mixed fabrics should be washed as for the fibre requiring the most care. For example, nylon and wool — wash as for wool, nylon and cotton — wash as for nylon.

*Nylon fur fabrics.* Although washable, it is wiser to have these fabrics dry-cleaned.

### Dry-Cleaning

Most stains will wash out with soap and water if treated immediately but if they are allowed to dry into the fabric they will not wash out so easily and stronger measures have to be taken. The usual dry-cleaning agents found in a household, such as carbon tetrachloride, trichlorethylene, benzene and petrol may be used with care. When taken to the cleaners the fabric must be clearly labelled 'nylon' so that it can receive the right treatment.

## WASHING POLYESTER FABRICS

This fabric is as strong when wet as it is when dry and soiling is easily washed out.

*Heat.* Polyester resists steam and heat better than most other synthetic fibres but it will melt at $260°C$.

*Acids.* It is resistant to those acids most commonly used in laundrywork.

*Alkalies.* It is not harmed by most cold alkalies but hot caustic alkalies will damage the fibres.

*Bleaches.* Unharmed by oxidizing bleaches.

### General Washing Rules

1) Wash by hand or machine in hot water, using any normal soap or detergent, but do not boil as creases may be difficult to remove.

2) Rub concentrated soap or detergent very gently on to dirty spots.

3) Rinse well and shake off surplus moisture because the fabric does not absorb it, or roll it in a towel. Avoid creasing the fabric and hang it to drip-dry, smoothing creases out while it is wet. DO NOT SPIN-DRY when hot as this causes creases to form. Fabric made from filament yarn dries very quickly at normal room temperature, but when it is made from staple yarn it holds more moisture and may take a little longer.

4) When ironing is necessary use a WARM iron — a steam iron gives good results. When polyester is mixed with another fibre, e.g. polyester and wool worsted, wash for the more delicate fibre, in this case wool.

## WASHING ACRYLIC FABRICS (ACRILAN, COURTELLE, ORLON)

*Heat.* Acrylics are very sensitive to heat and can distort very easily if washed in water which is too hot. Never use boiling water.

*Acids.* Safe to use at room temperature.

*Alkalies.* The fabrics are moderately resistant to alkalies.

*Bleaches.* Oxidising bleaches can be used.

### General Washing Rules

1) Use hand-hot water and soap-flakes or synthetic detergent. When soap is used, hard water must be softened.

2) Do not squeeze. Extra dirty parts can be sponged gently with concentrated detergent.

3) Rinse three times.

4) May be spin-dried for ten seconds only if the garment is COLD. Do not tumbler-dry.

5) Hang up to drip-dry and smooth out any creases while the fabric is wet.

6) If it is necessary to iron the fabric use a COOL iron and press lightly. Never iron Courtelle jersey when damp or use a steam iron.

### Bonded Fabrics

Wash for the weaker fabric, for example, tweed bonded to nylon, wash as for wool.

### Laundering Elastane Fabrics

Elastane yarn is not used by itself but always with another fibre so that both have to be considered when washing fabrics. If care-labels are supplied follow the directions, otherwise hand wash in hand-hot water, roll in a towel to remove as much moisture as possible and hang up to dry. Drying is fairly quick.

## WASHING STRETCH FABRICS

1) Wash by hand in hand-hot water using good quality soapflakes or detergent.
2) Do not use chlorine bleach as the fabric could retain it as chloramine which decomposes during ironing. This could cause the fabric to become scorched or discoloured.
3) Press with a very cool iron (lowest setting). On no account stretch the fabric while pressing, because heat will set in the extra stretch.
4) If care-labels are supplied follow the washing instructions on them carefully. When there are no instructions at all have the garments dry-cleaned.

## WASHING P.V.C.-COATED FABRICS

As the P.V.C. is on the outer side of the fabric, it will only need sponging with warm water. Do not iron the fabric as the P.V.C. may be damaged. DO NOT DRY CLEAN. The underside can be gently scrubbed in soapy water.

## WASHING COURLENE

The fibre is quite non-absorbent and resists acids and alkalies. Wash it by moving about in warm soapy water and then wipe dry.

## WASHING LACE

Wash lace according to the fibre from which it is made, i.e. cotton, wool, silk, rayon, nylon, polyester, etc.
1) Knead it gently in lukewarm water and soapflakes or synthetic detergent. Never wash in a washing machine or spin-dry.
2) Rinse very thoroughly in cool water and press out surplus moisture by rolling in a towel.
3) Iron on the wrong side over a thick pad so that the pattern will be well raised on the right side. The temperature of the iron will depend on the yarn.

## WASHING FABRICS WITH LUREX THREAD WOVEN INTO THEM

Lurex needs no special washing therefore the fabric should be laundered as for the basic yarn, but use a cool iron for pressing.

## WASHING FLOCK-PRINTED FABRICS

1) Wash in warm water without rubbing.
2) Neither wring nor spin-dry but hang up to drip-dry or roll in a towel.
3) Use a moderate iron and press on the wrong side over a pad.

## WASHING SPECIAL FINISHES

### Durably Pleated Fabric

1) Do not use a washing machine or spin-drier. Wash by hand dipping the fabric up and down in the water.
2) Hang up absolutely wet to drip-dry.
3) It should not need ironing but sometimes the pleats look more crisp if they are very carefully pressed with a cool iron.

### Crease- and Shrink-resist, Minimum Iron and Drip-dry Finishes

Do not boil.
Do not use bleach or starch.
Do not wring or spin-dry. Hang up to drip-dry.
Should require little, if any, ironing. If touching up is necessary, use a moderate iron.

### Permanent Sheen, Glaze, and Lustre Finishes

Wash according to the yarn.
Neither bleach nor starch.
Neither rub nor twist.
Press out moisture without wringing or spin-drying.
Iron while rather damp, with a hot iron for cottons and a moderate one for rayons, on the right side.

### Non-shrink Finishes

Wash normally according to the fabric.

### Permanently Embossed

These fabrics can be washed in a washing machine but when laundering by hand do not rub or twist.
Do not use bleach or starch.
Press the moisture out without wringing and do not use a spin-drier.
When the article is dry press it lightly on the wrong side but do not slide the iron over the fabric.

### Stain-Resistant and Water-Repellent Finishes

Wash normally for the fabric but do not use starch.
Hang to drip-dry.
Press under a damp cloth.

### Showerproof Finishes

These are best dry-cleaned.

### Flameproofed Fabrics

Wash normally in hot water. A washing machine can be used and also a spin drier.
Do not starch.
Iron while slightly damp.

### Calpreta Wonder Dry and Carefree Wringable

Fabrics with these finishes can be boiled, drip-dried or spin-dried and wrung and
will require very little ironing.

## AGREED WASHING AND IRONING TEMPERATURES

Firms who make fibres, firms who make the fibres into fabrics, firms who make
up the fabrics and those who distribute them all, together with the manufacturers
of washing machines, irons and detergents, have formed a Home Laundering
Consultative Committee to reach an agreement on general safe washing and
ironing temperatures based on the following code:

Wash tub: The washing process

Triangle: Chlorine bleaching

Iron: Ironing

Circle: Dry Cleaning

## The Washing Process

| | MACHINE | HAND WASH |
|---|---|---|
| **1** / 95 | Very hot to boil / maximum wash | Hand-hot or boil |
| | Spin or wring | |

White cotton and linen articles without special finishes

| | MACHINE | HAND WASH |
|---|---|---|
| **2** / 60 | Hot / maximum wash | Hand-hot |
| | Spin or wring | |

Cotton, linen or rayon articles without special finishes where colours are fast at 60°C

| | MACHINE | HAND WASH |
|---|---|---|
| **3** / 60 | Hot / medium wash | Hand-hot |
| | Cold rinse. Short spin or drip-dry | |

White nylon; white polyester/cotton mixtures

| | MACHINE | HAND WASH |
|---|---|---|
| **4** / 50 | Hand-hot / medium wash | Hand-hot |
| | Cold rinse. Short spin or drip dry | |

Coloured nylon; polyester; cotton and rayon articles with special finishes; acrylic/cotton mixtures; coloured polyester/cotton mixtures

| | MACHINE | HAND WASH |
|---|---|---|
| **5** / 40 | Warm / medium wash | Warm |
| | Spin or wring | |

Cotton, linen or rayon articles where colours are fast at 40°C, but not at 60°C

| | MACHINE | HAND WASH |
|---|---|---|
| **6** / 40 | Warm / minimum wash | Warm |
| | Cold rinse. Short spin. Do not wring | |

Acrylics; acetate and triacetate, including mixtures with wool; polyester/wool blends

| | MACHINE | HAND WASH |
|---|---|---|
| **7** / 40 | Warm / minimum wash | Warm / Do not rub |
| | Spin. Do not hand wring | |

Wool, including blankets and wool mixtures with cotton or rayon; silk

| | MACHINE | HAND WASH |
|---|---|---|
| **8** / 30 | Cool / minimum wash | Cool |
| | Cold rinse. Short spin. Do not wring | |

Silk and printed acetate fabrics with colours not fast at 40°C

| | MACHINE | HAND WASH |
|---|---|---|
| **9** / 95 | Very hot to boil / maximum wash | Hand-hot or boil |
| | Drip-dry | |

Cotton articles with special finishes capable of being boiled but requiring drip drying

| HAND WASH |
|---|
| See garment label |

Articles which must not be machine washed

Do not wash.

Chlorine bleach may be used.

 Do not use chlorine bleach.

## Ironing Temperatures

HOT (210°C)     Cotton, linen, rayon or modified viscose.

WARM (160°C)     Polyester mixtures, wool.

COOL (120°C)     Acrylic, nylon, acetate, triacetate, polyester.

DO NOT IRON.     This means DO NOT IRON and not that ironing is unnecessary.

## Dry Cleaning Symbols

(A)     Normal goods dry cleanable in all solvents.

(P)     Normal goods dry cleanable in perchloroethylene, white spirit, Solvent 113 and Solvent 11.

(F)     Normal goods dry cleanable in white spirit, and Solvent 113.

Do not dry clean.

Most fabric manufacturers supply 'sew in' labels giving the name of the fabric and instructions for its care and washing, so that, when buying fabric to make up, one should ask for a label and stitch it in somewhere noticeable — for example inside the back of the neck of a dress. Should the fabric not be washable, the label acts as a guide to the dry-cleaner. Even though the garment may be laundered at home it is easy, in the course of time, to forget from which fabric a particular dress is made.

In order to avoid confusion it should be mentioned here that some blended fabrics may be supplied with a label giving a higher setting than the above suggested recommendation. When this happens it means that tests which have been carried out on the fabric have shown that a higher temperature can be used safely. Likewise labels for cottons with special finishes may give a lower setting than is usually required for untreated cottons.

If the fibre is not known the lowest temperature should be used, that is 40°C. When washing man-made fibres the following points are important:

1) Wash often so that the articles do not get dirty enough to require hard rubbing.

2) Make sure that soapflakes and detergents are quite dissolved before putting the garments in and do not use more than is necessary.

3) Washing powders and detergents must be used only as the makers direct and if man-made fibres are not mentioned in the instructions do not use them.

4) Follow the makers' directions absolutely when using washing machines and wringers.

5) Wash, rinse and dry as quickly as possible but do not dry white fabric by heat or in strong sunlight as it may become yellowed.

6) Do not hang knitted articles up to dry while they are heavy with water for they may become distorted.

7) Always iron on the wrong side.

8) Always tell dry-cleaners what the fabric is.

## STORING FABRICS

### Cotton and Linen

Wash and dry very thoroughly. The drying is very important because if these fabrics are put away at all damp they will be attacked by mildew. Summer dresses can be rolled up rough-dried — that is without ironing — and put away in a drawer for the winter. Always put them away in a dry place otherwise they will pick up moisture from the atmosphere.

### Silk, Wool and Fur

Wash the articles or have them dry-cleaned and air them very well. Store in polythene bags, but make quite sure first that there are no holes whatever in the bags and close the tops very securely by folding over several times and fixing them with rubber bands or tightly tied string. If the fabric is free from moths when it goes into the bag it should be quite safe. If the smell is not objected to, moth balls may be put into the bags as a further precaution.

## Man-made Fibres

Viscose and acetate fabrics should be washed very clean and stored in drawers or in polythene bags. Moth grubs should not attack these fabrics but if they are put away soiled the grubs will eat the dirt and in doing so damage the fabric.

The other synthetic fibres are mothproof and need no special care during storage.

## Lace

Wash and dry well. Store in polythene bags or tissue paper.

# Index

# Index